Wooden Spoon
The children's charity of rugby

RUGBYWORLD
Yearbook 2018

EDITOR
Ian Robertson

PHOTOGRAPHS
Getty Images

Published in the UK in 2017 by
Lennard Publishing, an imprint of
Lennard Associates Ltd,
Mackerye End,
Harpenden, Herts AL5 5DR
email: orders@lennardqap.co.uk

Distributed by G2 Entertainment
c/o Orca Book Services
160 Eastern Avenue, Milton Park
Abingdon, OX14 4SB

ISBN: 978-1-78281-809-0

Production editor: Chris Marshall
Text and cover design: Paul Cooper

The publishers would like to thank Getty Images for providing most of the photographs for this book.
The publishers would also like to thank Andrew Beacham, Fotosport UK, Fotosport Italy, Inpho
Photography, World Rugby, Chris Thau and Wooden Spoon for additional material.

Printed and bound in Italy
by L.E.G.O. S.p.A

CONTENTS

We have a great sporting culture here at Norton Rose Fulbright, and we want to help make sure every child can enjoy sport. As rugby fans, we are particularly delighted to support Wooden Spoon through our corporate responsibility programme in London.

We believe that every child should have the chance to thrive in life, and so our charitable agenda across the whole of our legal practice focuses on improving opportunities for children and young people who are disadvantaged – whether physically, mentally or socially. I am proud to support Wooden Spoon, whose personal values so closely match our own.

Our focus is on local organisations where we feel we can make a real impact and benefit the communities in which we work. As well as providing funds for Wooden Spoon, we also encourage our people to participate in volunteering and fund-raising initiatives.

I wish everyone at Wooden Spoon a rewarding year ahead, and I would like to thank every person involved for their ongoing dedication and devotion to disadvantaged and disabled children in the UK.

Peter Martyr
Global Chief Executive
Norton Rose Fulbright

At Artemis, we are deeply aware of our broader responsibility to society and aspire to make a positive difference to the environment and communities in which we work and live. We have been doing so since 2007, when the Artemis Charitable Foundation was founded. Each year the firm gives a proportion of its revenues to the foundation, which manages our charitable activities and our involvement in the wider world. We encourage our people to develop their expertise and professional knowledge, both through formal training and through self-development. We then encourage them to share their skills through involvement in the various charities and causes we support; such as fundraising, volunteering and visiting the charities at work.

Artemis is delighted to support Wooden Spoon again this year and the work they are doing. This is our sixth year supporting the charity and we believe the opportunities the charity provides are pivotal to transforming the lives of many disadvantaged children. The inspirational values of Wooden Spoon, namely passion, integrity and teamwork, resonate strongly.

For the game of rugby, The British and Irish Lions tour to New Zealand made 2017 a very special year. In turn, this great book reflects on the team spirit and sportsmanship shown to the world by both teams; summed up by those wonderful words "Wow…This is rugby!"

From all of us at Artemis, we would like to thank everyone at Wooden Spoon for their dedication and devotion to disadvantaged and disabled children. Thank you.

Richard Turpin
Partner
Artemis Investment Management LLP

FOREWORD

by HRH THE PRINCESS ROYAL

BUCKINGHAM PALACE

Wooden Spoon's vision is to give every child and young person, no matter what their background, access to the same opportunities. The charity is inspired and motivated by its rugby heritage and with the tireless support of volunteers and the rugby community, it continues its vital work to transform the lives of children and young people with a disability or facing disadvantage.

Wooden Spoon uses the power of rugby to support a wide range of projects that are not just rugby focused; we provide sensory rooms, specialist playgrounds and sports activity areas to respite and medical centres and community based projects. Since its formation in 1983 Wooden Spoon has distributed in excess of £24 million to more than 650 projects, helping more than one million children and young people with disabilities or facing disadvantage across the UK and Ireland.

The core values of passion, integrity, teamwork and fun drive the ethos and spirit in everything the charity does. With more than 400 committted volunteers raising funds in local communities, Wooden Spoon is proud to say that the money raised locally is used to fund projects in the local area.

As Patron of Wooden Spoon I wish everyone involved great success and enjoyment through your fundraising efforts. I would also like to thank you for your dedicated interest and enthusiasm. This a unique and vibrant charity that will continue to achieve a lot more with your support, changing children's lives through the power of rugby.

Changing lives...

We fund life-changing projects across the UK and Ireland, using the power of rugby to support disadvantaged and disabled children.

Wooden Spoon is a registered charity in England and Wales (Reg No: 326691) and in Scotland (Reg No: SC039247)

Registered with FUNDRAISING REGULATOR

Who we are

Wooden Spoon is a grant making charity founded in 1983. Since then we have been committed to helping improve the lives of disabled and disadvantaged children.

We are one of the largest UK funders of respite and medical treatment centres, sensory rooms, specialist playgrounds, sports activity areas, and community-based programmes and have so far granted over £24 million to these fantastic projects. Inspired and motivated by our rugby heritage and by working together with the rugby community, with the support of its top sporting heroes, we have been able to help over 1 million children and fund over 650 projects.

In 2011 Wooden Spoon became the first charity to receive the Spirit of Rugby Award from the International Rugby Board and in November 2013 became the official charity partner of the Rugby League World Cup.We are also honoured to have HRH The Princess Royal as our Patron.

Find out more at
woodenspoon.org.uk

The story behind Wooden Spoon

A wonderful legacy emerged in 1983 after five England rugby supporters went to Dublin to watch England in the final game of the Five Nations Championship against the Irish. The game was lost 25-15 and England finished last in the table with just a single point gained from their draw against Wales.

After the match, in a Dublin bar surrounded by celebrating Ireland supporters, the five England supporters sought some consolation only for three of their Irish friends to present them with a wooden spoon, wrapped in an Irish scarf on a silver platter as a memento of England's dismal season.

Accepting the gift with good humour and grace, the England fans resolved to hold a golf match to see who would have the honour of keeping the wooden spoon.

Just a few months later the golf match was held and in the course of an entertaining day an astonishing sum of £8,450 was raised. The money was used to provide a new minibus for a local special needs school, Park School. This was to be the of first many Wooden Spoon charitable projects that has grown to over 600 in the years since. From defeat on the rugby field, and a tongue-in-cheek consolation prize, the Wooden Spoon charity was born.

Our Royal Patron
Our Royal Patron is HRH The Princess Royal who gives generously of her time.

Our Rugby Patrons
The IRFU, RFU, WRU, SRU, RFL all support us in our charitable work.

Sporting Partners
We work closely with a variety of clubs, league associations and governing bodies who help us achieve our vision of improving young lives though the power of rugby.

Wooden Spoon is a registered charity in England and Wales (Reg No: 326691) and in Scotland (Reg No: SC039247)

Craig's story

When Craig* was asked to leave home at 16 by his mum, his life was heading in a downhill direction. Craig's mum felt unable to cope, as Craig drifted further into spending time on the streets, taking drugs and hanging around with a bad crowd.

Placed in a children's home, Craig was feeling stuck in life. He was desperate for independence but couldn't see a way of being able to support himself. He became more frustrated and bitter about his future.

Thankfully, just when things were looking very bleak for Craig, he found crucial support through a special Wooden Spoon funded project – HITZ.

With their help, Craig was given the support he needed to develop a focus and learn life skills in order to support himself. The programme enabled him to get involved in education again, learn employability skills and boost his mood and self-esteem through rugby.

Craig secured himself a job with the local council; he now lives in his own accommodation and has a great support network. He has even started rebuilding a relationship with his mum.

The money you raise can help many young people living in desperate situations turn their lives around, and in turn, make a positive impact on society.

The money you raise can help many young people living in desperate situations turn their lives around, and in turn, make a positive impact on society.

*Names and specific circumstances have been changed to protect the identity of the young person.

Wooden Spoon is a registered charity in England and Wales (Reg No: 326691) and in Scotland (Reg No: SC039247)

woodenspoon.org.uk/membership

#wearerugby

FUNdraise for local children...

Join schools, colleges and rugby clubs across the UK & Ireland to raise vital funds for children and young people in need living in your community.

Join in today!

Wooden Spoon is a registered charity in England and Wales (Reg No: 326691) and in Scotland (Reg No: SC039247)

w: **woodenspoon.org.uk/schools**

t: **01252 773720**   e: **charity@woodenspoon.org.uk**

Join our club!

Become a member of Wooden Spoon for just £5 a month and help us change children's lives.

Members can:

- Win rugby tickets
- Hear from our projects
- Get a free gift
- Receive our bi-annual magazine

And most importantly, you will be helping change the lives of children and young people with disabilities or facing disadvantage across the UK & Ireland.

Wooden Spoon is a registered charity in England and Wales (Reg No: 326691) and in Scotland (Reg No: SC039247)

  Registered with **FUNDRAISING REGULATOR**

woodenspoon.org.uk/membership

#wearerugby

COMMENT
& FEATURES

1

Knocking at the Door
THE CASE FOR SIX NATIONS REFORM

by **CHRIS FOY**

World Rugby are striving to engineer greater opportunities for leading Tier Two nations such as Georgia against the strongest countries, but they cannot demand an upheaval of the Six Nations format

With every passing year, the clamour grows and evidence mounts. The thorny issue of Six Nations reform will not go away; in fact, it sits ever higher on the agenda as Georgia keep banging hard on a locked door. In a financial sense, there is no case at all. The annual championship is a resounding triumph in so many ways. It is the box-office gift that keeps on giving. Arenas are packed, revenue flows in

and ancient tribal hostilities are renewed against a backdrop of fervent public interest. But in purely sporting terms, there has been an increasingly hollow feel, in certain respects.

Rugby's showpiece northern event has become a cosy club. Year on year, the same six countries go through the old round-robin routine, without any threat to the status quo. The Wooden Spoon is a symbol of failure for the team finishing bottom of the pile, but the stigma does not come with a fall from grace attached. Promotion and relegation are dirty words in the corridors of power around the Home Unions and those of France and Italy – the last-mentioned in particular. In their 18 seasons among Europe's elite, the Azzurri have wound up in last place 12 times, but their participation has never been in any doubt – at least in the eyes of officialdom.

Yet, many of those who follow the sport, but do not have the right to decide on its structures, have grown infuriated by the absence of any meritocratic movement. This shift in public opinion has taken place in line with Georgia's emergence as a new northern force. The progression has been evident over a sustained period. A dozen years ago, the 'Lelos' were twentieth in the global rankings, while Italy were far ahead in eleventh. Four years later, Georgia had climbed to seventeenth, and in 2013 they were up to sixteenth. Now, they lie twelfth, while the Italians have slipped below them in the World Rugby chart, to fourteenth.

Despite having their Rugby Europe Championship (formerly the European Nations Cup) crown snatched from them by rivals across the Black Sea Romania this year, there is no escaping the conclusion that Georgia have outgrown their familiar surroundings. They have won the second-tier competition in eight of the last ten years. It has been an emphatic monopoly. Romania's feat in 2017 was to raise their own game to match and eclipse the team from Tbilisi, to promote their own case for upward mobility. But the establishment are happy to sit in their ivory towers and throw crumbs. The Six Nations 'blazers' want to retain a ring-fenced

ABOVE CJ Stander touches down for his first try on the way to a hat-trick in Rome as Italy are thumped 63-10 at home by Ireland in the 2017 Six Nations.

FACING PAGE Georgia celebrate victory over Tonga at Kingsholm in the 2015 World Cup.

competition – they don't want to make any concessions in the name of expanding their sport. The bigger picture and wider health of rugby won't stand in the way of the quest for profit.

Chief executive John Feehan was derided earlier this year for saying: 'It is a closed competition between the six countries, owned and controlled by the six unions concerned. There is no vacancy. I'm not saying we will never change, but at this stage, talk of bringing in other teams is premature.

'World Rugby have no input into this tournament. They have no control over it, no ownership of it. It is up to us, as the six unions, to run it as we see fit. It is World Rugby's job to develop the game; our job is to run the Six Nations.

'Do the unions have a responsibility to help develop and expand the game? Probably, yes, but should that go as far as messing with the most important tournament for all of them? Probably not.'

World Rugby are striving to engineer greater opportunities for leading Tier Two nations such as Georgia against the strongest countries, but they cannot demand an upheaval of the Six Nations format. So those on the outside continue to be left with noses pressed against the glass, looking in at the glitzy show while taking some comfort from the clamour on their behalf. It became very loud this year, on behalf of Georgia. They have taken over from Argentina as the game's hard-luck story; the country whose star is on the rise but lacking a home – at least in tournament terms. They most certainly have a home in a literal sense. Their bigger matches are played in front of 55,000 sell-outs in Tbilisi. Rugby is the national sport and the Lelos have the backing of a billionaire benefactor, as well as their people.

They hosted this year's World Rugby U20 Championship, and a generation of dazzling backs are emerging to complement their fabled legions of huge, imposing forwards. France's Top 14 league is awash with mighty Georgian props, but there is a clear ambition to broaden the set-piece-based repertoire with more running flair.

In June, a tour of the Americas by the senior side yielded Test victories over Canada and the USA, and Milton Haig – Georgia's Kiwi head coach – is adamant that his men are worthy of a shot at the big time. 'It's time to open the doors,' he said. 'Rugby's in Georgia's psyche. These guys are warriors. They've been farmers who have had to defend their land from invasions for thousands of years. Our scrum half, Giorgi Begadze, was fighting the Russians in South Ossetia in 2008. Rugby to them is a controlled war; a war they are pretty good at winning.

'Old people here would never have thought Georgia could be in the Six Nations in their wildest dreams. It would be the signal that Georgia, finally, have stepped out of the shadow of their big brother, Russia, to stand on the world stage by themselves.'

Yet, for now, the prospect of any meaningful reform is remote. The promotion-and-relegation debate will rage on, without becoming a likelihood. One-up, one-down play-offs are another option, similarly ignored. Turkeys will not vote for Christmas – certainly not any time soon. In the meantime, Georgia will keep up the pressure, Romania will keep them on their toes and others on the European fringes will press on with their rugby development programmes. The sport is taking hold in Spain, where 35,000 attended the domestic cup final in 2017, ahead of next year's Champions Cup final in Bilbao. Meanwhile, World Rugby have targeted Germany as a market full of potential, with investment and talk of a professional franchise in due course.

But there is still much work to do, as Rugby Europe – the continent's governing body – acknowledge, amid their perennial crusade to instigate a Six Nations revamp. Octavian Morariu, the organisation's president, said: 'The Six Nations could support European rugby more, but they don't. Staying in a rich, old-boys' club is not the answer. It's a very arrogant answer. Saying, "We are rich, thank you very much and we don't need you" is not consistent with the values of our sport.

'But there is support for change within the Six Nations – within those unions. Two or three years ago, these discussions would have been impossible, but now there are a lot of people listening. If we really want to develop European rugby, it won't be developed by the current system.'

That system is fostering stagnation, at a time when rugby should be aiming for dynamic expansion. The clamour will continue – louder and louder. Change is essential. The cosy club cannot survive indefinitely, when a more vibrant and varied future beckons.

ABOVE Georgia (in white) went down 45-29 to Argentina on their 2017 summer tour but picked up wins against Canada and the USA.

FACING PAGE Scrum half Gela Aprasidze on his way to a solo score for Georgia against Ireland in the 2017 WR U20 Championship in Tbilisi.

We are delighted to be supporting Wooden Spoon and would like to thank everyone for their dedication and devotion.

If you would like to find out more about Artemis, please contact your financial adviser, call 0800 092 2051 or visit artemisfunds.com.

ARTEMIS
The PROFIT Hunter

Brave New World
PRO RUGBY AND KATY MCLEAN

by **SARA ORCHARD**

Life as a professional eventually became easier but there was no hiding from the fact that being a Sevens player was all about being selected for Team GB at the Olympics

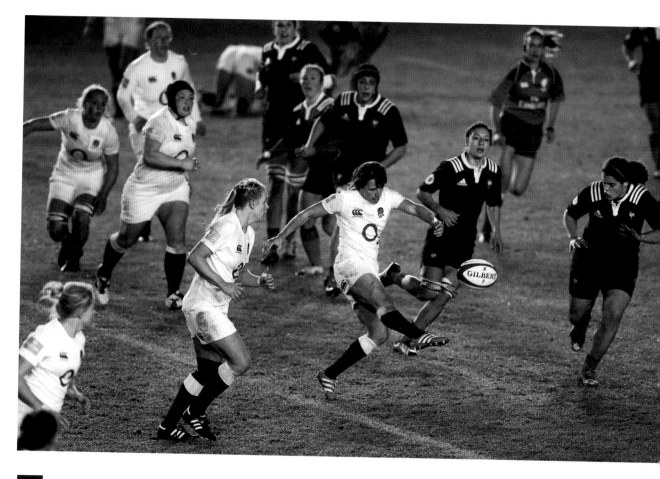

Three years ago, Katy Mclean went down for breakfast to find her face on the front and back pages of nearly every national newspaper. It wasn't expected but it was welcomed; she had just captained England Women to their first World Cup title in 20 years.

The 21-9 victory over Canada at the Stade Jean-Bouin in Paris was just another step in a six-month period that would transform her life. Having been hidden away in a Paris hotel, Mclean thinks the whole squad were innocent of what was to come next: 'We knew there had been an interest at home but we never expected it to be as big as it was – it was just phenomenal.' Cue the welcome home party at Twickenham, a trip to Downing Street to meet the Prime Minister and then a trophy tour.

Just as the South Shields teacher was trying to settle into a new primary school term, life changed again. The RFU announced it would be handing out professional contracts to its women players for rugby Sevens ahead of the Rio Olympics: 'I was 28, almost at the back end of my career and with it being Sevens specific, I thought I don't think I'll be in that mix.' She was very wrong: 'To be asked to be contracted and leave school to relocate to London – having only won the World Cup two months earlier – it was just a massive blur.'

The contract offer capped an incredible six months for Mclean, who had also picked up an MBE earlier in the year for services to rugby, and she laughs recalling the period: 'From going to Buckingham Palace to get my MBE, to going to the World Cup captaining my country, to becoming a professional rugby player – it was just like wow, how do I top this in my life?'

By early 2015, reality struck. The move to London saw the world champion struggle with life as a professional: 'It was an interesting journey. I had a massive issue relocating south to the point that I sat down with [England Head Coach] Simon Middleton and he said "Do you really want to do this – is this for you?"

'Remember I was from the era where we had always worked and rugby had been underlying – it hadn't been everything. And then it WAS everything.'

She was helped by living with England players Emily Scarratt and Natasha Hunt and laughter surrounds all talk of their domestic routine: 'Scaz [Scarratt] cooks everything – and that makes life a lot

BELOW Katy Mclean parading the World Cup at Twickenham along with other members of the victorious England team in 2014.

FACING PAGE Mclean the GB Sevens player at the Deodoro Stadium in Rio during the build-up to the 2016 Olympic Games.

PAGE 21 Fly half Mclean kicks for position against France at the Twickenham Stoop in November 2016.

easier. Mo [Hunt] is very tidy and likes to clean, so I brought very little to that party. When we relocated to Bisham Abbey we moved in with Kay Wilson and we became a four. Kay and I are very similar in that we're both rubbish in the house and offer very little. The others would mock us and say we'd stand in the technical area of the kitchen.'

Life as a professional eventually became easier but there was no hiding from the fact that being a Sevens player was all about being selected for Team GB at the Olympics. When 2016 arrived and selection was only a few months away she was thrown a curve ball by the coaches: 'I'd played a bit of ten, a bit of nine, and then Richie Pugh came in, the forwards coach, and he was saying I think you might be better as a forward – basically we want to look at you as hooker.

'It was like learning a completely new role, maybe three or four months out from Rio. There were also lots of people playing there, Heather Fisher, Rachael Burford, Amy Wilson Hardy, all almost six months longer than me. That was a challenge, but you just throw yourself into it and think all I can do is give this my best shot and see what happens.'

Mclean impressed, and then excelled. She won a plane ticket to Rio as the Olympics welcomed rugby Sevens to the programme for the first time. However, a smiling Mclean admits she had 'not a clue' when it came to the scale of an Olympic Games.

'You have these ideas of what an Olympic Village might look like but until you walk into something like that – it was absolutely crazy. It's literally like walking into a mini town.'

She fondly remembers the likes of Usain Bolt and Mo Farah being mobbed at breakfast, yet it was the more casual meetings with other Team GB sports stars that stick: 'We got a lift one day with Louis Smith, then a lift back with Jamie Murray, it was surreal. People in our GB House were really friendly, you see them as the big stars but when you're in the lift with them just chatting about your performance and how's it going, people are just normal.'

On the pitch Team GB's women had to swallow the hurt of finishing fourth as Canada won their bronze medal match: 'Yes, fourth was hard and it was painful, but to be part of something so much greater was for me a very humbling experience.

'When you are in rugby the World Cup is isolated to rugby and you forget there is a wider world. That's the beauty of the Olympics because you're part of something so much bigger.'

Now 31, Mclean is preparing for her third Fifteens World Cup in Ireland and chuckles as I ask if she'll consider trying for the Olympics in Tokyo 2020: 'Sevens is going to be for the younger kids, I'll be there watching.' However, her ambitions for the growth of the sport continue. In 2017 the RFU became the first national governing body to give out professional contracts to its women players in the 15-a-side code*; that's where Mclean wants to see bigger change on a global level: 'You'd like to see all international teams full-time or at least some kind of part-time.

'I think for us sometimes the hardest thing to hear is the only reason we [England] are doing as well is because we're full-time. Actually most of our [Fifteens] girls have only been full-time since January, but you want a level playing field. That way when you play each other you know that actually you're the best because everyone is having the same opportunity.'

Women's rugby is unrecognisable from when she made her international debut ten years ago, and Mclean knows her fortunes have been transformed by the changes. Fans can continue to enjoy the fruits of that evolution every time she pulls on a shirt, but when the talented footballer does call it a day she will be classed as one of rugby's most treasured players – skilful, adaptable and fearless. An amateur world champion but a professional pioneer. Enjoy her right boot whilst you can.

*The RFU subsequently announced that they would not renew the contracts of the 15-a-side squad but will in future direct their funding towards the seven-a-side game.

BELOW Vice-captain Mclean in action for England against New Zealand in November 2009. Her conversion and dropped goal helped England to a 10-3 victory over the Black Ferns, who were world champions at the time.

The Finest of his Generation
A PORTRAIT OF SERGIO PARISSE

by **MICK CLEARY**

There have been many great players in the game down the generations, all blessed with prodigious talent, but none of them can compare to Parisse in terms of taking punishment and coming back for more

Sergio Parisse is fluent in Italian. And English. And Spanish. And French. He is the man who not only plays a great game, he can speak one as well. To hear Parisse conduct a press conference is a mirror image of the multi-layered figure that he is on the field. The Italy captain is a man for all seasons, rugby's Renaissance individual, capable of great feats, endowed with all the skills of a modern-day player.

Parisse covers both ends of the spectrum: deft yet tough, nuanced but also a master of the basics, freewheeling yet ramrod straight on the forward drive, able to offload with the aplomb of a Sonny Bill Williams yet never shirking his duties at the coal face, chiselling inches as well as roaming free in the outside channels.

Parisse cuts a fine figure, with a noble bearing and celebrity catwalk looks. But for all that we can see in the flesh, the ability to bring his skills into play even under ferocious pressure, it is what we can't see that defines him best. He is a fighter, able to absorb pain not just of a physical nature but most importantly of the mental sort. There have been many great players in the game down the generations, be it a Gareth Edwards or a Philippe Sella or a David Campese or a Jonah Lomu, all blessed with prodigious talent, but none of them can compare to Parisse in terms of taking punishment and coming back for more. Parisse has shone in adversity, time and time again. He has never faltered, never let his head drop or his standards slip even though it has invariably been in a losing cause. He has played 126 Tests for Italy, the vast majority of them ending in defeat. Yet he has always risen from the canvas, still intent on delivering a knockout blow himself. Even last season, which opened with humiliating back-to-back losses at home to Wales (33-7) and Ireland

(63-10), and ended with a Wooden Spoon, Italy a long way adrift of the other teams at the bottom of the table with a points deficit of 151, Parisse was able to say during the tournament that: 'When I pull on the jersey I have the same emotion as when I was 18 years old.'

There are fears for the future wellbeing of Italian rugby after yet another traumatising experience in the championship. The clamour for promotion and relegation to be introduced grows ever louder. But Parisse remains proud and defiant. He plays, as he says, with the same dignity and ferocity as he did when he first came into the ranks of the Azzurri shortly after they were admitted to the Six Nations in 2000, making his debut as an 18-year-old against New Zealand in 2002. It was former All Black wing John Kirwan who took the bold decision to pick him, having no qualms about pitching in the youngster against some of the world's best. That match in Hamilton ended in a 64-10 defeat, a portent of trials and tribulations to come.

If Parisse had been born a New Zealander and played for the All Blacks, there is no doubt that he would be acclaimed as one of the greatest ever to have pulled on the silver fern. But never once has Parisse bemoaned his lot, the son of Italians, born in La Plata in Argentina where his father, also Sergio, once a well-regarded wing for L'Aquila, was based for his work with Alitalia. Never once has there been even a hint of self-pity that he has had to scrap away while others in different countries have been able to feed off the enhanced skills of their team-mates. Quite the opposite.

Admittedly, there was a sense that Parisse might have been drawing to the end of his time under former Italy coach Jacques Brunel, but when Conor O'Shea was hired to replace the Frenchman, Parisse committed himself to the rebuilding project, praising 'the vision of the future' that the former Harlequins director of rugby had

BELOW Destructive: Sergio Parisse and Maxime Mbanda haul down Scotland's Finn Russell at Murrayfield during the 2017 Six Nations.

FACING PAGE ... and creative: Parisse with ball in hand against England at Twickenham.

ABOVE Where it all began. Debutant Parisse chases New Zealand's Christian Cullen across the Hamilton turf in June 2002.

RIGHT Skipper Parisse and head coach Conor O'Shea in conversation at a Six Nations press event in Rome in January 2017.

brought to the post. 'I want to leave a legacy [myself] and give to Italian rugby a lot of things on the field,' said Parisse. 'This group is behind Conor and the whole coaching staff and will change Italian rugby. The road is long and hard but we will succeed.' The admiration was mutual. 'What is Sergio's legacy to the jersey?' mused O'Shea. 'If a greater player than him ever pulls on the Italian shirt, we will have the best player who has ever played the game.'

O'Shea needed Parisse to stay at the helm to buy time while he began the reconstruction programme that is so badly needed in Italy. Parisse was left out of the summer tour so that he could recharge properly for the 2017-18 season and a possible fifteenth Six Nations Championship.

There is little doubt that Parisse's athletic prowess will wane at some point given that his thirty-fourth birthday was in September. Yet he has the ability to influence a game no matter how parlous the situation. As England defence coach Paul Gustard said of him when preparing to face him: 'There are enough examples in his illustrious career that he can pull rabbits out of the hat. We have to be aware something can happen, something dangerous that is not there with an ordinary forward. He's always looking to do something different. There has to be a heightened awareness whenever he gets the ball.'

That has been true throughout his career. Parisse was completely on board with the rope-a-dope Italy adopted for the match against England at Twickenham in 2017 when it was decided not to contest rucks, a ploy that flummoxed the home side for well over an hour. Parisse led the charge, all too aware that Italy had

to scrap 'til their last breath if they were to withstand a title-bound side following their own pitiful start to the championship. Whatever it takes.

Parisse's relish for the fray has sometimes spilled over the fine line of legality. He has served suspensions for gouging as well as verbal abuse. Whatever his indiscretions, there is no doubt that he is seen as a warrior to be respected by his adversaries and not just a fancy ball-playing forward.

The more challenging the circumstances, the better he seems to perform, as ex-England lock Tom Palmer, his one-time team-mate at Stade Français, once told the *Daily Mail*: 'It seems as though he raises his game every time he plays for Italy. He often plays well for Stade, but not quite as consistently well as he does for Italy. He's the captain, it's a big responsibility for him and he rises to the challenge. He delivers every time he plays for them.'

And continues to do so, a man to be saluted, a player to be revered, the finest of his generation.

NEXUS

WE GO FURTHER

As specialist healthcare and education industry advisers and investors we provide a range of business and management services, including:

- Property fund management
- Real estate advisory services
- Corporate finance advice
- Private equity services
- Event management:
  International Opera Awards

HARRY HYMAN and

NEXUS

are pleased to support Wooden Spoon

The UK Rugby children's charity

Property Management

 Primary Health Properties

Corporate Finance

Media

HealthInvestor UK

EducationInvestor Global

HealthInvestor Asia

CODE

Moving business over the line

For more information visit:

nexusgroup.co.uk | phpgroup.co.uk | healthinvestor.co.uk | healthinvestorasia.com
operaawards.org | educationinvestor.co.uk | code-london.co.uk

Sevens Conquers the World
A HISTORY OF THE SHORT GAME

by CHRIS THAU

A youthful England side, captained by Andrew Harriman and coached by Les Cusworth, surprised the pundits and themselves by winning the inaugural event against a nominally stronger Australian team in the final

ABOVE The Melrose side who won the first rugby Sevens tournament, held at their club's home ground, The Greenyards, in April 1883. Melrose beat local rivals Gala in the final.

It is 134 years since the game of seven-a-side rugby was born in the little town of Melrose, southeast of Edinburgh, in the Scottish Borders. The local club Melrose FC, formed in 1877 by a group of disgruntled former Gala FC members, who broke away from the parent club in Galashiels, nicking the goalposts in the process, was in dire financial straits. In an attempt to raise much needed cash, the

Melrose committee decided to hold an athletic meeting, or sports day, at the end of the season, at which football (as the game was called at the time) was to be played alongside a number of athletic events including foot and dribbling races, place- and drop-kicking competitions etc.

The way the decision to hold a Sevens tournament was reached and by whom, as well as the format of the tournament, has been lost in the mists of time. It is said that during the discussion, most likely in the club committee, the then club skipper David Sanderson, the local butcher, and his apprentice Edward 'Ned' Haig, who played half back, recalled a tournament played with reduced numbers, in which they had partaken, on the English side of the border. The solution became obvious – a reduced format tournament, with teams formed of seven players, playing for 15 rather than 80 minutes. For the record, the first tournament was held on 28 April 1883, though with only six of the seven guest clubs turning up: Gala, Selkirk, St Cuthbert's of Hawick, Earlston, Gala Forest (a junior club from Galashiels) and St Ronan's Innerleithen. Gala and Melrose reached the final and the local club won after extra time.

The 'Sports' concept inspired the hard-pressed treasurers of the Scottish Borders clubs as the short game spread steadily throughout the region. Unsurprisingly, it was Melrose's arch-rivals Gala who picked up the challenge and launched their own tournament the following year. Equally predictably, they won their tournament, defeating Melrose in the final. A year later, not to be outdone, Hawick Sports kicked off with 16 entries, the largest tournament at the time, with their English guests Tynedale FC picking up the winners' medals. Tynedale FC, formed in Corbridge, near Hexham, in 1876, have won the Northumberland Cup 23 times in their long history, though arguably their greatest claim to fame is being the first English club to play and win a seven-a-side tournament anywhere in the world. Their astonishing sequence of success in the 1880s (in Galashiels, Hawick and Melrose) confirmed that Sevens expertise was not confined to the Scottish side of the border.

The fourth Borders club to launch their own Sevens tournament before the turn of the century was Jed-Forest in 1894, with Hawick taking the honours. In 1908 Langholm followed suit, the fifth club in the Borders to embark on a Sevens path before the Great War. Four more Borders clubs started their own Sevens after the war: Selkirk in 1919, Kelso in 1920 and Earlston and Peebles in 1923. Originally split into two Sevens circuits, in the spring and autumn, the Borders Sevens tournaments are now part of a 'Kings of the Sevens' series, played in April-May each year.

The 1920s saw a period of brisk expansion of the short game both in the rest of Scotland and in the north of England. It was Percy Park RFC who organised the first Sevens tournament in England, in 1921 at North Shields, an event conspicuously missing from the club's history pages. The North Shields tournament was followed by Rockliffe and Northumberland in 1922 and the Carlisle FC Sevens in 1923.

The way the short game reached New Zealand is not known, but some Scottish connection linking the Borders and Dunedin could be the answer, as the local union became the instigators of Sevens rugby in New Zealand. It was a charity tournament to raise funds for the local hospital, played at Carisbrook at the beginning of October 1889 in front of 1000 spectators, that started the ball rolling. It involved ten local clubs, with Dunedin FC defeating Dunedin High School 4-3 in the final. The second competition was organised by pioneers of New Zealand rugby Nelson FC, who ran a charity Sevens tournament won by the club's team captained by All Black George Harper. A big tournament involving teams from 28 clubs and schools in Manawatu in 1920 is mentioned by New Zealand rugby historian Bob Luxford. However, somehow the short game failed to reach an elevated status among New Zealanders, who perhaps rightly regarded it as a kind of fun game to be played before and after the main season.

In Argentina, where expatriates introduced rugby in the 1870s, Sevens was launched by the River Plate Rugby Union, the forerunner of the UAR, at the initiative of Buenos Aires Football Club in 1921. Eighteen clubs entered the pioneering event, won by the host club who defeated Belgrano Athletic 11-10 in the final. In Samoa, it was the Marist Brothers who imported the short game from New Zealand, in one of the periodic surges of interest in Sevens during the 1920s. The archives of the now defunct Apia Rugby Union have been lost, but the late Samoa Union official and national team manager Tate Simi confirmed that Sevens had been part of the domestic Samoan scene for a long time.

The 1920s is also the likely period in which the Fiji Sevens romance started, as confirmed by historian Jeremy Duxbury, who referred to an article in *The Fiji Times and Herald* of 1926 suggesting a Sevens tournament as the way forward. The records are virtually non-existent, but a 2015 article in *The Fiji Times* describes the Catholic brothers at Naililili in Rewa as early pioneers of Sevens in the 1940s; perhaps they started earlier. We don't know when the Suva Union Sevens started, but we are told that in 1956 the legendary Josefa Levula led the Army B team who beat the Police A in the final. The launch of the Marist Sevens in Suva in 1976 coincided with Fiji's ascent onto the world scene as a powerhouse of rugby Sevens.

Edinburgh-born Dr J.A. Russell-Cargill, a passionate Sevens supporter since his days with the Edinburgh Academicals, convinced the committee of the Middlesex Union to support his initiative to launch a seven-a-side tournament open to all London clubs at the end of the season. The RFU approved the project and the world famous Middlesex Sevens tournament was born at Twickenham in 1926. Although the Middlesex Sevens involved several dozen clubs from the county and London, the biggest seven-a-side tournament in the world remains the Rosslyn Park Schools Sevens, launched in 1939 by the late journalist Charles Burton, the founder of the Public School Wanderers, which gathers, every year, over 7000 schoolboys and schoolgirls between the ages of 13 and 18 from the UK and overseas.

Appropriately, the first ever international rugby Sevens tournament was held at Murrayfield in 1973, to celebrate the centenary of the Scottish Rugby Union. Somewhat prophetically, it was England, captained by a burly Loughborough Colleges prop by the name of Fran Cotton, who won the '73 tournament, leaving in their wake a star-studded Welsh side captained by the legendary Gareth Edwards, the hosts and Sevens specialists Scotland led by Gala's man Peter Brown, New Zealand captained by Alex Wyllie, Australia with Peter Sullivan as captain, France led by Victor Boffelli, and a President's Seven, which included South African stars Piet Greyling and Jan Ellis. In the final the English Sevens team defeated (22-18) an exciting, never-say-die Irish side captained by Mike Gibson.

> **BELOW** Lawrence Dallaglio heads for the try line in the inaugural Rugby World Cup Sevens final, as England beat Australia to win the title.

GREENE KING
IPA
INDIA PALE ALE

PROUD PARTNER OF
WOODEN SPOON

GREENE KING IPA
THE PERFECT
MATCH PINT

ENJOY
RESPONSIBLY
WWW.ENJOYRESPONSIBLY.CO.UK

Legend has it that the novelty and the excitement of the Sevens displayed at Murrayfield inspired two spectators from Hong Kong looking for a suitable tournament format to launch in the then colony. It is also said that the Melrose factor – smaller squads and a short time – played a significant role in their decision to make Sevens the game of choice of the HKRFU. With South African businessman 'Tokkie' Smith at the helm of the HK Union, the Hong Kong International Sevens was born three years later in 1976, and after several lean years – when it battled to make ends meet – it finally became the 'Koh-i-Noor' of the world Sevens circuit in the mid-1980s.

As the Sevens game took the world by storm (with several dozen tournaments in the USA alone), at the initiative of the Scottish Union the IRFB launched the Rugby World Cup Sevens at Murrayfield in 1993. A youthful England side, captained by Andrew Harriman and coached by Les Cusworth, surprised the pundits and themselves by winning the inaugural event against a nominally stronger Australian team in the final. Four years later in Hong Kong in the second RWC Sevens, the dazzling magicians from Fiji led by Waisale Serevi beat South Africa in the final to take the Melrose Cup – nicknamed 'Meli' – to Suva. New Zealand, featuring the game's superstar Jonah Lomu, secured the 2001 RWC Sevens crown in Argentina, while Fiji led by the one and only Serevi bounced back, winning 'Meli' again in Hong Kong in 2005. By then, the ailing international Sevens game, threatened by the pressure of professional rugby, had been rescued, reinvigorated by the newly launched IRB Sevens World Series, a circuit of ten major tournaments which commenced in 1999-2000. It was the late IRB chairman Vernon Pugh who argued strongly among his peers for the launch of the World Sevens Series, foreseeing the potential of the short game to bring rugby back into the Olympics.

BELOW One of the Sevens greats, Waisale Serevi, gives New Zealand plenty to think about in the final of RWC Sevens 2005 in Hong Kong as Fiji win the Melrose Cup for a second time.

Rugby Characters
JOHN IRELAND'S CARICATURES

by **ADRIAN STEPHENSON**

In 2002 John Ireland was asked to provide a caricature for the Wooden Spoon Society Rugby World yearbook. For the next 15 years he contributed a 'rugby character' to each new edition

As an aspiring commercial artist John Ireland had never been particularly interested in sport, but at the beginning of the 1980s things were about to change. With a growing reputation as a caricaturist, John was commissioned to illustrate *To Horse To Horse*, a book written by Terry Wogan and based on the racing tips that he gave, with the aid of racing journalist Tony Fairbairn, on his breakfast show. This meant a new experience for John – a day at Newmarket observing the racing fraternity. John's illustrations were a great success and the same publisher asked him to create a portfolio of *Cricket Characters* in a book for which Christopher Martin-Jenkins would provide the words.

John now found himself watching cricket on television as part of his research and there was even the occasional visit to Lord's. Other books of sporting characters followed – golf, snooker, racing – and in 1990 *Rugby Characters* was published by Stanley Paul with text by Cliff Morgan.

Further rugby prints were commissioned by the Leeds-based company run by Charlie Parker and former England scrum half Nigel Melville. These included a popular limited edition print of Will Carling's 1991 Grand Slam team signed by all 15 players.

John Ireland prints became popular auction items at rugby events, and in 2002 John was asked to provide a caricature for the *Wooden Spoon Society Rugby World* (now *Wooden Spoon Rugby World*) yearbook. For the next 15 years he contributed a 'rugby character' to each new edition.

John has laid down his pen, put aside his paints and is now enjoying retirement, still following sport and doing all those things for which there had previously been no time. The next few pages provide a gallery of the rugby characters that he created for *Wooden Spoon Rugby World* from 2002 to 2016.

RUGBY
CHARACTERS

CARICATURES BY JOHN IRELAND

TEXT BY
CLIFF MORGAN

ABOVE The cover of *Rugby Characters*, John Ireland's first excursion into rugby in 1990.

RIGHT Martin Johnson, the first 'character' to appear in *Wooden Spoon*.

FACING PAGE (clockwise from top left) Lawrence Dallaglio, Tana Umaga, Jason Robinson, Sébastien Chabal.

Eastdil Secured

is proud to support

Wooden Spoon Rugby World

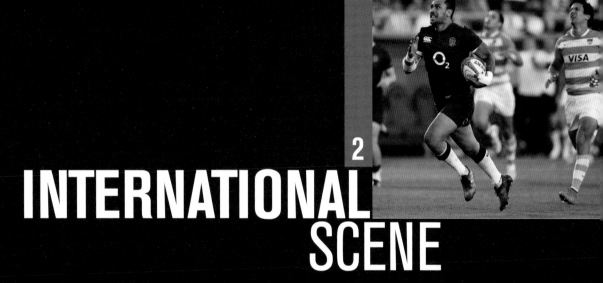

INTERNATIONAL SCENE

2

Wallabies on the Brink
AUSTRALIAN RUGBY IN DISTRESS

by RAECHELLE INMAN

What may not be obvious to the other rugby-playing nations is that in Australia rugby is the smallest of the four codes of football. AFL, soccer and rugby league are better organised, better funded

When New Zealand is your closest neighbour, it means that the All Blacks become the yardstick against which you measure your performance. This wouldn't be particularly good for any team's confidence, but it is especially difficult when the consensus is that the team in question is facing its demise. The Wallabies have not held the Bledisloe Cup – the symbol of trans-Tasman rivalry – since 2002. This year the Wallabies have not only been beaten by the Kiwis (as Australian rugby fans have come to expect), but the Aussies were also defeated at home by Scotland. This was unexpected. Frankly, Wallabies fans expect a win against the Scots, especially with Scotland's best players in New Zealand with the Lions. This shines a light on the dire state that is Australian rugby in 2017.

Most of the relevant measures of success (win/loss ratios, viewership, attendance, finances, participation at junior and club level) are not currently looking healthy for Australian rugby. How did it come to this? A perfect storm has been brewing for years.

The Australian Rugby Union (ARU) decided to actively court rugby league players, who had no real passion for – or loyalty to – rugby union. Players included Mat Rogers, Lote Tuqiri, Wendell Sailor, Timana Tahu and Andrew Walker. This was a marketing ploy to increase the appeal of rugby union against the other codes, particularly targeting rugby league fans. The consequences of this approach from the rugby union management were significant. Firstly, it bled budget from the ARU's coffers to invest in other players – and other priorities – and it didn't meet the desired objective of broadening the game's fan base. Not surprisingly, very few of these league players made a particularly good transition to union and they didn't stay long. Secondly, a clear message was sent to up-and-coming rugby union players at schoolboy and club level that they weren't relatively valued; some players decided to switch to other codes or go overseas. The traditional pathway was not clear any more. Finally, long-term loyal rugby fans grounded in supporting the clubs that grow and develop future stars of the game became disillusioned and started to lose their connection to the national side.

What may not be obvious to the other rugby-playing nations is that in Australia rugby is the smallest of the four codes of football by every measure. AFL (Australian Rules), soccer and rugby league are better organised, better funded and as they compete amongst each other, rugby's traditional domain is collateral damage. The media focus on, and access to, games of AFL, rugby league or soccer (locally

BELOW Mat Rogers (left) is congratulated by fellow rugby league convert Lote Tuqiri after scoring against Italy in Melbourne in 2005.

FACING PAGE Wing Julian Savea runs away to score as New Zealand win 37-10 in Auckland in October 2016 to retain the Bledisloe Cup.

and internationally) also isolates the dwindling portion of the population that supports rugby. Finally, it should be noted that increasing immigration is much less likely to be from rugby nations than historically was the case. Consequently, only a small proportion of Australia's youth dream of playing for the Wallabies, and this has led to a meaningful decline in participation numbers.

According to Roy Morgan Research, rugby union has fallen to the twenty-sixth most popular sport in Australia, with the same number of organised participants as ballroom dancing! The research reveals that 93,000 Australians have given up the sport over the past 15 years, with the number of rugby union players down to just 55,000. Football (soccer) is perceived to be safer by parents and is now the most played sport in Australia with 623,000 participants, a rise of 46 per cent compared to rugby union's decline of 63 per cent over the same 15-year period.

In the junior ranks, registering to play for a rugby union club is more expensive than the three other codes, which can be a barrier for families – and rugby is predominantly run by volunteer parents. Other codes are well organised by comparison, with paid development officers, administrators and coaches.

Schools in rugby strongholds are now offering, even promoting, AFL. Last year the goalposts were torn down from the main oval of the Sydney Church of England Grammar School (also known as Shore School) – one of the Great Public Schools (GPS) and the rugby nursery that produced Wallabies like Phil Waugh and Al Baxter – and were replaced with Australian Rules football facilities. It was a sign the goalposts had, quite literally, shifted. To combat this the Australian Rugby Union has launched the Game On primary school programme, which teaches the fundamentals of rugby and aims to broaden the base. Sixty per cent of the Game On programme has deliberately been positioned by the ARU in government schools to make rugby union accessible to a new audience, and the ARU is promoting this for both boys and girls. The strategy is clear: the ARU is trying to get the ball in the hands of more kids. It is free for participants as it is government-funded, but the Game On programme only runs for five weeks. The challenge is converting these kids to play in organised rugby union clubs outside of school and to manage 'churn' – retaining these kids as they grow, especially when the game shifts to contact.

Australia really needs to adopt weight levels for age categories, replicating the successful system New Zealand has had for many years. While it is not clear from the evidence that it makes the sport any safer, it would undoubtedly address the perception it is not safe. On this front, the ARU has introduced an 'age dispensation' policy where a player may play in the age group he or she is turning in the relevant calendar year and in the age group one year above.

As part of the strategic plan, the ARU has put a great deal of focus into pushing the new VIVA7S 'tackle-less' short form version of the game. Eight thousand five hundred have registered in the past 12 months and more than 40 per cent of participants are female. The thinking is that girls today are the mums of the future and this will spearhead the shift to a more diverse and inclusive game that better reflects the community in which it needs to thrive.

While the ARU is investing in programmes like Game On and VIVA7S, the bulk of the resources are being spent on a small group of existing 'leading' Wallabies, resulting in good national and Super Rugby players heading overseas to Europe and Japan in their prime and depleting the depth of Australian rugby. Compounding this is the active pilfering from the ranks of promising schoolboy rugby union players by rugby league clubs that are thirsty for talent. The NRL (National Rugby League) clubs can afford to put 15-year-olds on contract and take them out of rugby, before the rugby fraternity has mobilised to secure them.

Like any major issue, the first step to deriving a solution is that Australian rugby needs to admit there's a problem. This process has begun with former players starting to speak out. Brett Papworth has led the charge, presenting the ARU chairman with a letter signed by dozens of former Wallabies players and coaches articulating many of these issues and some proposed solutions. Some of the forthright excerpts from that letter include:

'Our deep concern is the total imbalance between what is spent at the top of the game, both on players and administration, versus what is allocated to the grass roots. This is unsustainable and a total disgrace.'

'History has consistently shown that volunteer armies win wars because they are motivated in heart and soul well beyond the rewards of mercenaries. There is a war going on in sport in Australia and the ARU's most vital asset, the grass roots players, coaches, managers, mums, dads and volunteers in all tasks required to run a club are being shafted by the ARU and the State Unions they oversee.'

Journalist and former Wallaby Peter FitzSimons wrote in his column: 'My chief hope is that the course taken is one of trimming the sails, of pulling back from grand visions of winning World Cups any time soon

– of even prioritising World Cup victories as the be-all and end-all – and instead setting ourselves for the long haul.

'This includes getting Wallabies connected back to the grass roots, so they care, and the grass roots know they care.'

This disconnect has led to a feeling amongst the rugby community that elite players have a lack of passion and no real incentive to win. The concern amongst them is that the hierarchy think it's better to focus on elite programmes, rather than using club rugby as a true pathway. When Australians look across the ditch to New Zealand, they see future All Blacks go through immersive, connected rugby pathways where they play countless club and regional rugby games to hone their craft and continue to be connected in a meaningful way to the broader rugby community.

In New Zealand the philosophy is that club rugby makes great players better. It is where they learn to understand the game. In July 2017 the local derby of the Warringah Rats v Manly Marlins in Sydney attracted a crowd close to 7500. The passion is certainly alive at this level and little, or no, money changes hands. These guys play for the love of the game and that is engaging for the fans. Rugby needs to harness this tribal passion to create a future.

If it doesn't, the trend for crowd numbers at professional games in Australia is likely to continue its rapid decline (the Waratahs were down almost 30 per cent this season on last year). Fans are not making the same effort to watch professional games. In addition to dwindling crowds, a national team that is losing has led to television ratings that have plummeted and corporate sponsors walking away at the end of their contracts.

Since the start of the professional era, significant sums of ARU investment have been put to short-term, ineffective solutions. FitzSimons said: 'An example is committing a reported $750,000 a year to giving David Pocock a sabbatical year, allowing him time off from the Wallabies, while keeping him secure for the 2019 World Cup.

'As fine a player as Pocock is, as crucial as he is to the Wallabies performing well, it is madness to pay that much money to one player, to not play – his only commitment this year is to do three, one-hour meet and greets with individuals of the ARU's choosing – all while the rest of the game is crying out for development officers, for resources, for fertiliser to make the grass roots grow.'

Another major decision that has contributed to today's reality was the ARU creating the Western Force in 2006 and the Melbourne Rebels in 2011 for expansion in Super Rugby. Both teams were located in Australian states with fiercely tribal and strong Australian Rules football cultures.

At the time, the Australian Super Rugby teams were reasonably competitive and the ARU was determined to shift rugby union to a national game, to compete against the larger codes. The unforeseen consequences of this rapid expansion were that this diluted the talent pool significantly, further bled the ARU of funds and led to a break in cohesion across the Australian teams. Data shows that teams who stay together consistently succeed, and Australian rugby has paid the price of frequent market movement across the five franchises and diluted depth in the talent pool.

BELOW The Australian Women's Sevens Olympic gold medal win in Rio provided much needed good news for the ARU.

The Force and Rebels sought instant success, lost money and cost the ARU a considerable investment to keep them alive. ARU chairman Cameron Clyne revealed that $28 million was spent propping up Super Rugby over the past four years, a staggering amount for an organisation that was already suffering financial stress.

The situation was compounded by SANZAAR's decision to increase Super Rugby again, from 15 to 18 teams last year, bringing in a sixth South African side as well as Argentina and Japan, to create a four-conference competition. Leading figures in the game warned the ARU the 18-team format would be detrimental to Australian rugby, but they agreed to it anyway, tempted by the lure of increased broadcast dollars, which vanished in propping up teams.

In 2012 the ARU had an opportunity to adopt the New Zealand model and start to align player management and coach management, to ensure an aligned quality of the coaching standards of the Super Rugby teams and the management of talent. Instead they decided to make the Super Rugby teams even more autonomous. This system is now entrenched and would be difficult to restructure. It is widely agreed that the number of Super teams needs to reduce. This will concentrate and align the talent, build unity, consistency and start the process of rebuilding the right culture.*

Former ARU CEO John O'Neill believes Australian rugby has much to learn from the approach of our closest neighbours. This excerpt is from a leaked email to Brett Papworth.

'Several years ago, post Rugby World Cup (RWC) 2007, the NZRU held a summit and the outcome was a non-negotiable priority #1 All Blacks to be #1 in the world, not sometimes but all the time! All the systems and processes they have since put in place, at all levels, are designed to achieve that objective. They created a Unity of Purpose! Result? Back to back RWCs and best in the world by some distance. Why have I referenced that? Well, that's what I think the ARU has to do. Emulate that Unity of Purpose. It must remove the obstacles which are the vestige of the federated model and embrace a purpose-built model for Australian rugby which is better than the Kiwi's!'

The ARU are two years into a five-year strategic plan which is underpinned by a vision 'to inspire all Australians to enjoy our great global game' and focuses on four key areas: making rugby a game for all; igniting Australia's passion for the game; building sustainable success in the professional game; and creating excellence in how the game is run.

The ARU seems to be channelling the limited budget that remains (after the elite player payments) into a focus on girls' and women's rugby. The Australia Women's Sevens team winning gold in Rio has been the one glimmer of hope for the ARU, a real fairy tale; but many are asking if this focus on females can drive the revival for the whole code. And how long will this take?

Australian rugby has access to limited resources and so it needs to be smart about how those resources are used. It starts with a clear objective: Australia wants to be the leading rugby nation in the world. It then needs to have a plan: the passion is at the grass roots. The passion must never be lost again. It drives player dedication, loyalty of supporters, a desire to participate from the moment you can tie up your boots – simply so that when someone pulls on the green and gold jersey they aren't doing it for the money, they are doing it for the honour of representing every single person at the grass roots, and for their country.

There are many clever, passionate and knowledgeable people in Australian rugby. All key stakeholders need to come together, put aside their individual agendas, and ensure a robust plan is established for the greater good of the game. Once you realise this you can justify: a sustained focus on, and real investment in, juniors, schools and club rugby; prioritising development officers and coaches; broadening female participation – all resulting in initiatives to revive the grass roots, creating true pathways and reconnecting those that don the Wallaby jersey (and the management) with the grass roots.

The Wallabies have a history of performing well on the international rugby stage, particularly in World Cups. They say things happen in cycles. We have been in hard times before. I sincerely hope Australian rugby is close to the bottom of this cycle.

FitzSimons wrote: 'Ladies and gentlemen, we are in for a long period of wet-weather football, sustained tough times that will need long-sprigs, limited ambitions, and satisfaction in moving the game forward by inches if necessary, just so long as it keeps moving. It will be one for the True Believers.'

The rugby faithful will have to be very patient and hopefully one day, in the future, Australia will return to an era when the Bledisloe Cup is genuinely a two-sided contest again. With ARU funding, a vibrant international game, and the enthusiasm of the people at the local rugby park, Australia has the ability to bring those days back. We just need leadership to deliver an aligned plan, nurture the right kind of culture and invest in the grass roots: passion for the game is born when you are a kid, passion makes good players great and equally establishes loyal, long-term supporters.

*Following a SANZAAR decision to reduce Super Rugby from 18 teams to 15 for 2018, South Africa withdrew the Cheetahs and Kings, who seem destined to join Europe's PRO12. In August the ARU announced that Western Force would be the third franchise to leave Super Rugby. However, at the time of writing, the fate of Force remains in dispute.

Blacklash!
THE WR U20 CHAMPIONSHIP

by ALAN LORIMER

In their final group game, New Zealand had a rematch with Ireland, and perhaps with memories of Manchester in mind the Baby Blacks inflicted a 69-3 dispiriting defeat

You might be forgiven for thinking the 12-team format of the 2017 World Rugby U20 Championship in Georgia consisted of New Zealand plus 11 other countries, so dominant were the Baby Blacks on the road to their sixth global title. It was a dominance that extended even to the final where New Zealand ran riot against the defending champions England to take the title with a record-breaking score of 64-17. It was a crushing defeat for the Six Nations champions but not unexpected given that the Baby Blacks averaged 55 points per match in the build-up to the final showdown.

All of which confirms that the New Zealand system, based on depth and intensity of competition, continues to churn out a steady supply of talented young players ready to fill the boots of current All Blacks when the cycle demands. Players like fly half Tiaan Falcon, sadly forced to miss the final because of a head knock sustained in the previous round, and the human battering ram that is hooker Asafo Aumua, a hat-trick scorer against England, are just two who will surely make the step up to All Blacks rugby. And you could pick a whole lot more ready to progress to the next level of New Zealand rugby. They are the stars in waiting and unless the rest of the planet can respond, then the All Blacks' grip on the global game looks set to continue.

It is not unreasonable to suggest that the genesis of New Zealand's 2017 championship win began 12 months earlier in Manchester when, in wet conditions, Ireland inflicted a rare defeat on the Baby Blacks in the pool stage, resulting in New Zealand, for the first time in the history of the tournament, missing out on a place in the top four. This year New Zealand were determined to avoid a Manchester malfunction and signalled their intention to return to the top of the rankings by blitzing through the Oceania Rugby U20 Championship a few weeks before competing in Georgia.

The Baby Blacks' dazzling teamwork established in the Oceania tournament was carried over into the World Championship. It was a blend of powerful forward play with audacious attacking rugby from a back line that had pulverising pace and handling skills of the highest order. It was a back line that contained stars of the future in full back Will Jordan and wingers Caleb Clarke and Tima Faingaanuku, a trio of strike runners. No less influential was scrum half Ereatara Enari and centre Orbyn Leger, and in the forward pack second-row Isaia Walker-Leawere and flanker and skipper Luke Jacobson, who has the commanding presence of a Richie McCaw or indeed any one from a line of distinguished All Black back-rower captains.

New Zealand wasted no time in displaying their title-winning credentials by defeating Scotland 42-20 in the first round of pool matches. Italy were next to succumb as the Baby Blacks steamed to a 68-26 win, the

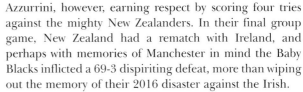

Azzurrini, however, earning respect by scoring four tries against the mighty New Zealanders. In their final group game, New Zealand had a rematch with Ireland, and perhaps with memories of Manchester in mind the Baby Blacks inflicted a 69-3 dispiriting defeat, more than wiping out the memory of their 2016 disaster against the Irish.

The semi-final match against France looked to be following a similar pattern after the Baby Blacks scored five tries without reply to lead 36-0 five minutes into the second half. Then, whether it was a switch-off by New Zealand or a sudden surge of self-belief by France, Les Tricolores produced arguably the best rugby of the championship to bag four tries and provide the only real challenge the young New Zealanders received in the entire tournament. France's fourth try, from Lucas Tauzin, brought the scoreline to 36-26 with 11 minutes of the match remaining. Could the French bridge the gap? '*Non*' was the answer as Falcon decided enough was enough of New Zealand's more relaxed approach in the second half by kicking a penalty goal, giving his side a 39-26 win and a place in the final.

The final was yet another New Zealand v England affair, the fifth such shoot-out between the two most successful countries at Under 20 level. England, however, never exhibited the same invincibility they had shown in Manchester 12 months earlier, and aside from a whopping 74-17 first round win against Samoa the defending champions had to work hard for their wins. In the second round Wales presented problems for England but ultimately the men in white aided by two spectacular tries from their star wing Gabriel Ibitoye emerged 34-22 winners over a Welsh side that scored three tries.

Then in their final pool match, England faced Australia in a winner-takes-all game that went down to the wire. The young Wallabies were quick out of the blocks, establishing a 16-3 lead by the end of the first quarter from a try by centre Sione Tuipulotu and accurate goal-kicking from scrum half Harrison Goddard. England, however, recovered and after tries by Ibitoye and prop Marcus Street, both converted by fly half Max Malins, it was advantage to the defending champions with the scoreline showing 17-16. Harry Nucifora then nudged Australia ahead with a penalty goal, but in the final act of this compelling drama Malins kept his cool to kick the winning points. That victory gave England a place in the semi-finals against South Africa, who had drawn with France in round one before achieving an unconvincing win against hosts Georgia. But if there were doubts about the ability of the 2017 Baby Boks, these were dispelled by a 72-14 annihilation of Argentina in the final match of Pool C.

The semi-final stage always produces an epic match and the England v South Africa game maintained this tradition. It was England who had the early momentum, building up a 17-7 lead through tries from their skipper and No. 8 Zach Mercer and scrum half Alex Mitchell and conversions and a penalty from Malins, only to be pulled back to 17-12 on half-time by a second touchdown by South Africa's powerful No. 8 Juarno Augustus. Then a try from second-row Ruben van Heerden and a second conversion from the Sharks full back Curwin Bosch put the Baby Boks in the driving seat. It seemed that South Africa were destined for a place in the final when Bosch put over a penalty goal for a 22-17 lead, but Mercer scored a late try under the posts leaving Malins to kick the winning conversion.

And so to the final. England were the clear underdogs, but by how much was the question. The answer was quickly made clear as New Zealand set about the destruction of England's best, with irresistible attack-from-anywhere rugby underpinned by power up front that gave the Baby Blacks a 40-7 lead at half-time. England's only statement of defiance was an early try by flanker Ben Earl. The second half only brought more misery as New Zealand piled on a further 24 points, but England, to their credit, still had the bottle to score tries by Mitchell and lock Josh Bayliss. New Zealand's tally of ten tries that included a hat-trick from Aumua and a brace by Jacobson said it all. After the final Jacobson admitted that New Zealand had eased off too much in the later stages of the penultimate round. He said: 'We definitely took our learnings out of the semi-final against France, so [against England] we were able to come out and put some good footy on show and hang on to our lead.'

BELOW England skipper and No. 8 Zach Mercer dots down for the opening try against South Africa in the first semi-final.

FACING PAGE Alan Tynan, Ireland's full back, on his way to the line against Georgia in the ninth-place play-off which the Irish won 24-18.

PAGES 48-49 Luke Jacobson, captain of New Zealand, lifts the trophy after his side's triumph in the final at Tbilisi's Mikheil Meskhi Stadium.

France and South Africa contested for third place and in the event it was the Baby Boks who prevailed. Still Les Tricolores gave hope that French rugby might be changing from the rigid forward play of the Top 14 to a more fluid game.

Among the Six Nations countries it was Scotland who made most progress. Having finished second bottom in the Six Nations Under 20 Championship, the Scots achieved a massive turnaround in Georgia by taking the fifth overall placing, their only defeat being against New Zealand. As a country with small resources, success matters to Scotland and certainly suggests a number of players are ready to make the step-up to the professional ranks. Several are already there, notably full back Blair Kinghorn who has played regularly for Edinburgh, skipper Callum Hunter-Hill and flanker Matt Fagerson, who have both had games for Glasgow. Hunter-Hill along with four-try scorer Darcy Graham have been signed by Edinburgh and it seems likely that others will follow to the two Scottish professional sides. Undoubtedly one of the stars for Scotland was Connor Eastgate, and given the scarcity of quality 'tens' in Scottish rugby the Wasps Academy fly half could find himself in Gregor Townsend's squad.

Scotland were in the same group as Italy, who surpassed expectations by playing effective and attacking rugby that gave them an overall best ever finishing place of eighth, providing hope for the future of Italian rugby. Also in the Scotland group were Ireland, who as the 2016 runners-up had to shoulder unrealistic expectations of similar success. Ireland's chances of making an impression on the 2017 championship crumbled long before the tournament began when it was learned that they would be without their talented fly half Johnny McPhillips along with five other front-line players. Ninth place, after defeating Georgia, may not have been their ambition but with 12 of their squad available for the 2018 tournament Ireland will surely recover.

For Wales, defeat to Scotland in the fifth-place semi-final meant that the Welsh side would have to play Italy in the final round. In the event Wales had to come from behind before winning 25-24. Within the Welsh squad, back-row Will Jones, prop Kieron Assiratti, centre Ioan Nicholas, and half backs Arwel Robson, Reuben Morgan-Williams and Dane Blacker seem poised for further honours.

Elsewhere, last year's bronze medallists Argentina provided the biggest shock after dropping from third to eleventh, their final game against Samoa providing a high-scoring thriller. Los Pumitas won and avoided relegation but it did not matter. Argentina will host the 2018 championship and thus automatically will be one of the 12 teams competing – alongside New Zealand, of course.

90 Not Out
THE STORY OF CZECH RUGBY

by **CHRIS THAU**

After the war the game was revived by a group of former players and enthusiasts who put the rugby balls found in a dungeon of Prague's Strahov Stadium to good use. New clubs sprang up

It was Czech painter, cartoonist and sports journalist Ondrej Sekora who fell in love with the game whilst in Paris in 1924. He was 25 at the time and an already accomplished artist, though there is no information about the circumstances of his sudden conversion to rugby, nor is there anything known about his rugby prowess. An apocryphal story claims that it was the matches of the 1924 Olympic tournament that made a great impression on him, but there is no evidence to support that. Suffice to say that after his return to Czechoslovakia he started to translate the laws of the game, creating the Czech language terminology in a booklet, *Rugby, how to play it and its rules*, which he published in 1926. In an attempt to expand the base of the game and the number of people understanding it, he also illustrated the laws with his drawings and published them in *Sports* magazine. The first rugby match organised by Sekora was held in Brno, the capital of Moravia, on 9 May 1926, with him as the referee. He selected the two teams, SK Moravska Slavia Brno

and AFK Zizka Brno, from local athletes and wrestlers, teaching the players how to play. It was a success and Slavia won 31-17. The rest is history.

Less than a month later in June 1926 Slavia Brno took on Vienna Amateurs RC, as it was cheaper to travel to the Austrian capital than to Prague, the match ending in a 12-all draw. Meanwhile, rugby was making inroads in Bratislava, the capital city of Slovakia, with the local club Slavia strongly supported by the British residents including the UK consul, a Mr Dowden. Sekora went on promoting the game as rugby slowly expanded in the country. The following May, the first rugby match in Prague was organised, a promotional venture between Slavia Bratislava and Moravska Slavia Brno, which led to the launch of SK Slavia Prague RC, as well as a handful of student clubs. In May 1927, the Romanian national team, on their way back home from France and Germany, made a stopover in Bratislava, where they defeated (23-6) a Czech selection which included Dowden and six other British players and a couple from Vienna Amateurs. Though the Czechs do not regard this as a full international, the Romanians do.

In 1928 the Czechoslovak Rugby Union was founded and a seven-club league was launched. In November 1931 the newly formed Czechoslovak national team travelled to Leipzig where they were beaten 38-0 by a very strong German team, while the return match in Prague in May 1934 ended with the visitors winning 19-9, which showed the considerable progress made by the hosts in such short time. In 1933, the Czechs played Italy twice, the first match in Milan, where they lost 7-3, followed by a game in Prague which they lost 12-3, not bad for a group of players who had started playing as a side less than two years earlier. The 1934 match against Germany ended the pioneering phase of Czechoslovak rugby as a combination of factors, from a shortage of funds and playing fields to the downright hostility of the powerful soccer lobby, forced the game into the wilderness.

After the war the game was revived by a group of former players and enthusiasts who put the rugby balls found in a dungeon of Prague's Strahov Stadium to good use. New clubs sprang up in Prague, as well as in Moravia and Bohemia, and in 1946 the British mission stepped in to help organise a tour for a British Army XV from Vienna. The British servicemen made a huge impression on their keen hosts with their elevated levels of skill and rugby know-how and helped the game spread further. The Czech Army adopted the game and at one stage had over 40 military teams competing in a services league. A visit by a Soviet ice-hockey coach who 'disapproved' of rugby led to the termination of the rugby programme in the army. These were the days when the 'Great Soviet Empire' led by example. However, the game prospered among students and young people and in November 1946 the re-formed Czech national team took on the Netherlands in the first post-war international, which they won 14-8 in the Dutch town of Bussum. In 1957, the Czechoslovak team went to Moscow to take part in a promotional tournament designed to kick-start rugby

in the Soviet Union, where they lost 38-19 to the full French side captained by Jean Prat and were beaten 12-11 by the Romania of Viorel Morariu – pretty good considering the game had been revived in Czechoslovakia only ten or so years earlier.

The ninetieth anniversary of Sekora's pioneering match of 1926 passed almost unnoticed by the outside world but for a brief trip to Prague by Barbarian FC, who took on the Czech national team at the Marketa Stadium in Prague in front of a record crowd of nearly 8000 spectators last November. It was the biggest rugby match in the Czech Republic since the game turned professional, and while the Czech Union and the Barbarians deserve full praise for the initiative, the 11-try drubbing (Barbarians 71, Czech Republic 0) revealed the unbridgeable gap between elite professional rugby and amateur athletes.

'This is the reality and we must face it and find ways to deal with it. We have to go back to square one and rebuild everything from the foundations,' said former Czechoslovakia captain and coach Eduard Krutzner, 'Medack' to his many friends and admirers and arguably the most enduring legend of Czechoslovak rugby. 'Before the advent of professional rugby we were quite competitive in Europe. At one stage in the 1960s we had a very strong team, which I captained. We played in the FIRA top division, holding our own against the likes of France, Romania, Italy and Spain. We were better than Spain at the time, beat Italy in Prague and drew nine-all with Romania, our oldest adversary. In fact I could say that for a while we were fourth on the continent, long before Georgia emerged from the rubble of the former Soviet Union. My most memorable match was in 1968 against the full French team, which included all their stars: Yachvili, Lasserre, Cester, Plantefol, Salut, Carrère, Puget, Lacaze, Bonal, Lux, Maso, Campaes and Villepreux … although we lost 6-19 in Prague we played exceptionally well,' he recalled.

An accomplished basketball and ice-hockey player, Krutzner made a swift and lasting impact in rugby with his skills, handling ability and athleticism, as well as his leadership qualities. Born in April 1935 in Prague, he played basketball for the Slovan Orbis club (with whom he won several national championship titles in the late 1950s), ice hockey for Pilsen, and rugby for TJ Prague, where he was coached by the legendary Jan Kudrna, father of Bruno Kudrna, who later succeeded him. Krutzner made his international rugby debut against the GDR (East Germany) in Zwickau in 1960, winning his forty-third and last cap against Morocco in 1972; for the last six years of his international career he was captain.

'In the 1970s, although we had lost a bit of steam due to the retirement of several veterans, we were still a force to be reckoned with. Bruno Kudrna, who was arguably one of the finest players to represent the country, started playing for the national team in the early 1970s, while I was still captain. We were funded by the government, but suffered from the habitual problems of non-Olympic sports in a communist society, which was obsessed with Olympic medals. We were under pressure to perform and I recall being suspended for three years from international competitions by our Stalinist sports minister Antonin Himl because we had had a poor season and lost all our matches. I remember Himl asking me how much steroids we needed to start winning matches. I told him what I thought of that, and as a result he kicked me out of the game,' Krutzner said.

Krutzner was the first of an extensive list of Czech players to have his talent recognised abroad. It was his outstanding ability in adverse circumstances that was noted by the Besançon talent scouts when France hosted Czechoslovakia in 1969 (France won 34-14 but were made to fight hard for every score, with Krutzner leading from the front) and he was invited to play for and coach the local Olympique club. It took a while until he received the relevant authorisation from the Czech communist authorities, but once arrived in Besançon, Krutzner played his heart out and made a significant contribution to the club's promotion to the French first division in 1972, a minor miracle still regarded as the highlight of the club's history. After his return to Prague, Krutzner started coaching his club TJ Prague, with whom he won seven national championship titles, while taking over the Czechoslovak national team in 1975. He was sidelined by the sports ministry, but then returned to rugby coaching after the fall of communism.

At the time, the game was fully amateur in Czechoslovakia so Bruno Kudrna, 'Brunka' to his team-mates, opted to stay in the country to develop his professional career in mechanical engineering, rather than go abroad in search of an outlet to enable him to fulfil his exceptional rugby talent. He became the architect of a Czech national team that punched well above its weight in European rugby and was voted player of the year six times. He became national coach in 1990, after a couple of years as Krutzner's assistant, having taken a degree in Physical Education to enable him to coach senior rugby teams. Born in 1951 in Prague, he learned the game under the stern regime of his father Jan Kudrna, the coach of his one and only club TJ Prague and a legend of the Czech game. The young Kudrna had a meteoric rugby career that saw him win 59 caps at fly half and centre between 1971 (when, with Eduard Krutzner as captain, he made his international debut in an unexpected 12-6 win against Spain in Madrid) and 1986, when Czechoslovakia, this time with him as skipper, defeated the Netherlands 24-12 in Prague. Strangely, two drawn matches are set vividly in his memory as the highlights of both his playing and coaching careers. 'As a player, I recall the three-all draw against Italy in Rovigo as probably the most significant match I played, though my debut against Spain two years earlier was equally memorable. It was for the first time in my career I played in front of such a big crowd [about 10,000 in Madrid], and all I remember is that I passed the ball three times to my wing Milos Hora, who scored three tries. We won 12-6 although we were very much the underdogs. As a coach my highlight was also against Spain, in 1990, when we finished 22-22 though we were 15-6 down at half-time. It was my first match as head coach and I made a few substitutions at half-time that changed the playing pattern and enabled us to draw in the end.'

RIGHT Bruno Kudrna, Czech international player and later national coach, pictured here in the colours of TJ Prague.

FACING PAGE Czechoslovakia v France, Prague, 1966. Home skipper Eduard Krutzner is third from the right; his counterpart Michel Crauste third from the left. The match ended in a 36-12 win for France.

In 1993, Bruno Kudrna was the coach of the Czech Republic team in the qualifying rounds of the 1995 Rugby World Cup. Having coached the U19 and U23 selections previously, he had launched a renewal project for the senior side, which unearthed several gold nuggets in the Czech talent mine. I recall him saying at the time: 'Having coached the U19s and U23s, I knew we had several talented boys that could go all the way: Vrba, Vlk, Skolar, Machacek, Sousek, to mention just a few. Machacek was a supremely gifted player, but I was trying hard to bring consistency to his game. One day he could be absolutely sensational, and the next simply awful. Vrba and Swejda were players of pedigree, but really we did not know how good they were, or how good the team was, for that matter. We do not have opportunities to develop players in a pressure environment. Our domestic league is too weak, and we are also short of quality coaches and referees,' he said at the time. 'The arrival of professionalism caught us totally unprepared in every respect. Society has changed and the majority of the players try hard to make a livelihood, while playing for pleasure,' he added a few years later.

Interestingly, Jan Machacek, one of the youngsters Kudrna mentioned in 1993, became the first Czech professional player to make an impact. Born in 1972 in Prague, Jan was playing for the family club Slavia Prague (where his father Dusan used to play), when he decided to find out more about himself and the world of rugby, leaving for New Zealand to join Dunedin Pirates for a season. That was in 1995, the year the game turned professional. By 1997 he was

BELOW A star is born. Young Jan Machacek (left in red), pictured during an RWC 1995 qualifier against Israel in 1993.

FACING PAGE Three heroes of Czech rugby. From left to right: Bruno Kudrna, Eduard Krutzner and Martin Jagr.

a fully professional player with Newport in Wales, voted the supporters' player of the year and making a name for himself in European rugby. 'He was the fastest No. 8 I had the pleasure to play with; a very good player, and an even better guy,' former Newport team-mate John Colderley recalled. After Newport, Machacek played for Sale and then Pontypridd, ending his professional career with the current French champions Clermont Auvergne, where he spent two seasons. 'That was the highlight of my career – it was a great environment, playing and training with top international players, coached by top coaches and striving to better yourself all the time. I still regard Tim Lane as the best coach I worked with,' he confessed. He played for the Czech Republic in a total of 55 matches, the last against Hong Kong in 2009, and was assistant national coach after he stopped playing.

Another Czech player to establish himself as a top professional in the competitive French rugby set-up was winger Martin Jagr, born in 1979 and schooled at the Prague club Sparta. After a season with Pontypool in 2000, he joined Toulon in 2001, where he played for eight consecutive seasons, moving to pastures new in 2009, two years after Mourad Boudjellal acquired the club. Surplus to requirements in the team of 'galacticos', he joined the Bordeaux Bègles club, where he spent two more seasons, followed by a transfer to Stade Montois in 2011. After Jagr, the production of rugby professionals capable of playing at the top European level slowed down, though prop Lukas Rapant and veteran lock forward Miroslav Nemecek did not do too badly for Oyonnax in the Top 14. The painful truth is that despite its obvious potential and traditions, Czech rugby, in its ninety-first year, has been left behind, as proved by the demolition at the hands of the Barbarians. A fully funded professional franchise in Prague should be able to exploit the considerable athletic potential and reinvigorate the dormant Czech game.

Blitzboks Streak to the Title
THE HSBC WR SEVENS SERIES

by **PAUL BOLTON**

South Africa put down an early marker by winning the series opener in Dubai. They trounced New Zealand 40-0 in the quarter-finals and beat Fiji, the 2016 winners and Olympic champions, in the final

In the course of lifting their fifth title of the season in the penultimate leg in Paris, South Africa's Blitzboks won the World Sevens Series for the first time since 2009 and broke the stranglehold of New Zealand and the Pacific Islands. It was fifth time lucky for South Africa, who had finished runners-up in the previous four seasons, and only the second time in 18 years that the title had not gone to either New Zealand, Fiji or Samoa. South Africa's success came in a season in which Sevens rugby benefited from increased profile and media exposure following the success of the format in the 2016 Rio Olympics, with USA and Canada also making encouraging progress under English coaches.

USA, with former England Sevens coach Mike Friday in charge, built on their sixth place in the previous two seasons to finish a place higher despite not winning any of the Cup competitions in the ten rounds of the tournament. But they did reach the final in Singapore where they were beaten 26-19 by Canada who claimed their first Cup title in their 140th leg of the Sevens Series. Canada, under the tutelage of former England Sevens defence and skills coach Damian McGrath, secured 22 points for their win in Singapore which helped them finish a creditable eighth in the final standings.

There could be no denying that South Africa were the best team over the course of a six-month season as they won half of the tournaments and their aggregate of 192 points has only once been bettered, by New Zealand in 2002 when the series was played over 11 legs. South Africa reached eight finals and only twice failed to progress beyond the quarter-finals in a punishing schedule which saw them zig-zag the globe. South Africa's win meant that Neil Powell, a member of the side that won the title in 2009, became the first man to win the series as a player and a coach. 'I am much more relieved now than I was in 2009 when I was a player. Back then I was just happy to win it, this time there is huge relief,' Powell said.

'We are extremely grateful and blessed. The team worked for this for three seasons. Last year we came close, but this time we managed to do it.

'I have to give the guys credit. They are an incredible group that never feared hard work and they deserved this title.'

South Africa, who were runners-up to Fiji in 2016, put down an early marker by winning the series opener in Dubai where they made easy progress through a group that included Uganda, USA and Scotland. They then trounced New Zealand 40-0 in the quarter-finals and, having disposed of Wales in the semis, beat Fiji, the 2016 winners and Olympic champions, in the final.

England checked South Africa's progress in Cape Town where they gatecrashed the hosts' party with a 19-17 win in the final. South Africa rallied with successive tournament successes in Wellington, Sydney and Las Vegas. Another defeat to England followed in Vancouver, Fiji took their revenge in the Cup final in Hong Kong, and South Africa missed out on the semi-finals in Singapore where they were beaten 19-17 by Australia in the quarters.

ABOVE Matías Osadczuk in action against New Zealand at the Vancouver Sevens in March. The young Puma was voted Rookie of the Year.

RIGHT 'Speed Stick' Perry Baker of USA cannot prevent Matt Mullins from scoring as Canada take their first title in 140 attempts.

South Africa clinched the series title in Paris after they had beaten New Zealand in the semi-finals. England's earlier defeat by Scotland meant that Philip Snyman's side could not be overtaken but they went on to beat Scotland in the final for good measure. The pressure was off when South Africa went to Twickenham where their hopes of another Cup success were ended by a 17-12 defeat by England in the quarter-finals when Dan Norton scored the winning try after the hooter. South Africa's success was very much a squad effort but Snyman, who made 158 tackles – the most in the series – and Werner Kok (145 tackles) were outstanding in defence and Seabelo Senatla led the attack with 32 tries and 40 clean breaks.

England, Wales and Scotland all improved on their 2016 placings, with England rising from eighth to finish as runners-up. Simon Amor's team won two Cups but again missed out at Twickenham where Scotland beat them in the final to retain that title. Norton became the leading try scorer in Sevens Series history when he scored his 245th in Hong Kong, overtaking Kenya's Collins Injera. Norton had extended his record to 261 by the end of the season.

Scotland's Twickenham triumph helped them climb three places to seventh, with Wales improving two places to tenth. Their semi-final appearance in Dubai was the high point of Wales's season; finishing fourteenth out of 16 in Hong Kong was the nadir. Wales captain Sam Cross pipped Norton to the DHL Impact Player of the Year Award, having made 101 tackles, 29 breaks, 63 offloads and 166 carries across the series.

Kenya, the surprise package of 2016, lost ground by dropping five places to twelfth and it was the two North American sides who were the

success stories this time. USA, who finished ninth in the inaugural Olympic Sevens, prospered despite being without Carlin Isles, the leading try scorer in Rio, who missed eight of the rounds because of injury. In Isles's absence USA relied more on Perry Baker, nicknamed the 'Speed Stick', and he responded by topping the series try-scoring and points-scoring tables with 57 tries – including eight at Twickenham – and 285 points.

Baker's sparkling form secured him a place in the series Dream Team alongside his compatriot Danny Barrett, South Africa pair Chris Dry and Rosko Specman, Fiji's Kalione Nasoko and Jerry Tuwai and Norton. 'We showed that we are a force to be reckoned with. The top teams in the world are well within our view,' said USA captain Madison Hughes.

Canada's form was more erratic than the United States as they failed to qualify for the Cup competition in four legs of the series. But they compensated for those failures with their stunning success in Singapore. Canada were beaten by Fiji in the pool stage but then sprang surprises to defeat New Zealand in the quarter-finals and England in the semis. In the final Canada led 19-0 at one stage but USA levelled at 19-19 in the second half before Lucas Hammond sealed victory and Canada's first Cup title with a last-minute try.

Canada had been stripped of their Olympic funding after failing to qualify for Rio but gave the sport back home a timely boost with their first series title. 'This is huge for Canadian rugby. We lost $1 million in funding, our Fifteens results have been poor, so this just gives us a shot in the arm. It's a big deal for us,' said McGrath, a Yorkshireman who previously coached Samoa.

Matías Osadczuk of Argentina was voted Rookie of the Year despite having his campaign cut short by a cruciate knee ligament injury sustained against Australia in Hong Kong. Despite Osadczuk's efforts Argentina had a modest campaign and dropped four places to ninth, with a 13-point haul in Wellington their best performance.

New Zealand, who had won 12 of the previous 17 World Series, also dropped a place to fourth, equalling their lowest ever finish in the competition. They twice finished third but failed to win any of the legs for the first time since 2009. Japan lost their status as a core team after a campaign which saw them scrape just 20 points. They were relegated for the second time in three years and will be replaced by Spain for the 2017-18 series.

The series attracted plenty of interest wherever the Sevens circus pitched its tent. More than 734,000 spectators watched the ten rounds, an increase of almost ten per cent, with a surge of interest in the format following its debut in Rio a likely factor in the rise.

Summer Tours
ENGLAND IN ARGENTINA

by **HUGH GODWIN**

Showing the finisher's panache, Solomona fended off Tuculet's head-on tackle, skipped infield, swatted Matías Moroni away and sprinted to the posts for an exultant finish, added to by Ford's conversion

Two Test matches with Argentina in upcountry venues were expected to be a severe examination of an England squad deprived of around 30 possible picks by injuries, suspension and the concurrent British & Irish Lions tour. In fact, aside from a few concerns about a leaky defence, the short summer trip to South America was a stunning success. England won both Tests, with four tries scored in each match and the solid performances of comparative old hands – the captain Dylan Hartley, Mike Brown, Danny Care, Jonny

May, Joe Launchbury and George Ford among them – embellished by eye-catching contributions from 11 debutants, from the Sale Sharks back-rower Tom Curry, whose nineteenth birthday fell between the first and second Tests, to the try-hungry recent convert from rugby league, Denny Solomona.

England settled into Buenos Aires with a reception at the British Embassy and a night out on which the No. 8 Nathan Hughes downed a huge Tomahawk steak, and might have had another if there had been no training next day. Then a two-hour flight took them west to arid San Juan, near the Andes, with its ten per cent humidity and a 25,000-plus crowd at the Estadio del Bicentenario. Whereas all the Argentina players had spent the first half of the year playing together for the Jaguares in Super Rugby, there were unfamiliar faces throughout England's first-Test squad of 23. The ten new caps awarded by head coach Eddie Jones was a figure last seen versus Wales in 1956.

A match eventually hailed as one of the most enthralling Tests in recent years kicked off with Mark Wilson, the flanker from Newcastle Falcons, penalised for not releasing after a tackle, and Argentina's debutant on the left wing, Emiliano Boffelli, got the riot of scoring up and running as he latched onto a left-footed grubber by fly half Nicolás Sánchez. Ford was joined in an attack-minded England midfield by Alex Lozowski of Saracens and Exeter's Henry Slade, with Jones having hired his Australian compatriot Glen Ella as temporary backs coach for the second summer tour running. A dozy ruck offence by Argentina prop Lucas Noguera gave Ford the kind of kick he has sometimes struggled to land consistently for his country, on a shallow angle about 50 metres from the posts. But the 24-year-old fly half struck the ball confidently and accurately and he would keep on adding crucial points from the tee.

Harry Williams of Exeter and later Harlequins' Will Collier were new men at tight-head prop for England, who regularly forced turnovers after the tackle, with Wilson a specialist in the art. One such steal led to a counterattacking try on 30 minutes, as Leicester's loose-head prop Ellis Genge made a typically ferocious carry, and Lozowski – watched by his dad Rob, a one-cap England centre from the 1980s – ran 30 metres before linking with Care, who had Brown and May supporting. Care resumed his involvement at a ruck and the scrum half's pass, while falling backwards, enabled Ford to put the scorer Marland Yarde over at the right-hand corner. Ford's conversion in addition to his earlier second penalty had England 13-7 up.

A try by Argentina's second-row Tomás Lavanini was converted by Sánchez, and a penalty by the latter made it 17-13 at half-time. But the best fun was yet to come. A Ford penalty was followed by a beautiful show-and-go from Slade to create a try for May similar to Boffelli's, which Ford converted. Then Solomona was introduced; calamitously at first. The Auckland-born wing lost his footing as scrum half Martín Landajo scooted past him from a scrum with Argentina cleverly outnumbering England in midfield, although the slip was compounded by the open-side Curry being handed off by Landajo before Jerónimo De la Fuente applied the finish. Straight from the restart after Sánchez's conversion, Argentina cut through Ford, Lozowski and the floundering Solomona for a wonderful long-range try by full back Joaquín Tuculet and a lead of 31-23 with 54 minutes gone.

Piers Francis, born in Kent but playing latterly for Auckland Blues, came on for Lozowski. Then two key moments involving Sánchez kept England in touch – a drop at goal that flopped wide and a penalty that flew wide after a withering Pumas scrum. Sánchez was

replaced by Juan Martín Hernández, just as Ford whacked over a penalty from near the halfway line.

Feeling good about himself, Ford next grabbed an Argentinian fumble and raced off, giving a pass to Francis and receiving one in return for a try and a scoreline of 31-31, with Ford's attempted conversion his only missed kick. Another Argentina error came as Hernández put the restart out on the full, and when the 34-year-old took a dropped goal rather than press for a try with 76 minutes played he left England, improbably, with a sniff of victory.

The tourists made the most of it with a thrilling try from a line out set up by Hernández's kick into touch a minute after his drop. The throw by Hartley on England's ten-metre line, on their left wing, was tapped down by Saracens' Nick Isiekwe to Exeter's Jack Maunder – two of the new faces, who had come on for Charlie Ewels and Care respectively – and Maunder launched the ball flat into the midfield where Ford looped round Francis, and May was tackled, but England held on. Sharp passes by the locks Isiekwe and Launchbury fed Francis, who in turn put the ball in Solomona's hands on halfway. Showing the finisher's panache that had brought him from Melbourne Storm and London Broncos to San Juan, via Castleford and Sale, Solomona fended off Tuculet's head-on tackle, skipped infield, swatted Matías Moroni away and sprinted to the posts for an exultant finish, added to by Ford's conversion. Another two mistakes by Argentina followed, as they strayed in front of the kicker to present England with a scrum feed and then allowed the set-piece to take so long to form, with Maunder cannily dawdling over the put-in, that the clock ticked beyond full-time. The tourists heeled the ball and kicked it dead to seal a celebrated victory by 38 points to 34.

Seven days later, it was a different scene in Santa Fe, an hour's flight north of Buenos Aires. There was raging heat – about 90 degrees Fahrenheit – and an old-style preamble with a joint press conference in a restaurant involving Jones, Hartley, Argentina skipper Agustín Creevy, head coach Daniel Hourcade and Julio Clement, the first player from the region to represent the Pumas, having been capped in 1987. Solomona wowed the locals by posing for selfies outside the England team's hotel, and even the water bottles bought by the fans were stamped with the date of the match.

The Estadio Brigadier General Estanislao López – known as the Elephants' Graveyard in tribute to giant-killing feats by the home football team Colón – staged another action-packed occasion, as England won

35-25. Francis was given the No. 12 jersey outside Ford, and the much-talked-about flanker Sam Underhill – newly signed by Bath from Ospreys – made a dynamic debut alongside the returning Chris Robshaw. Others in the squad were not so lucky, as the Northampton back Harry Mallinder and London Irish wing Joe Cokanasiga were among a number of players whose involvement never went beyond the training field.

A try for each team made for a lively opening eight minutes, as Ewels wrapped around from a line out to score from Ford's easy raid over the gain line. Then Tuculet danced between Yarde and Brown to score after Lavanini's initial scramble from a line out. It was 18-13 to England by half-time, with two penalties each by Sánchez and Ford, then a try for Francis on a beautiful counterattack made by Brown's mid-air interception of a Sánchez cross-kick. Twelve minutes after the break, a ricochet from a grubber by Francis gave Argentina's flanker Pablo Matera a try with footwork Diego Maradona would have been proud of, before another sally by Brown made a try for his fellow Harlequin, Care, and Ford kicked the conversion for 25-18. When Boffelli grabbed his second try in two Tests after De la Fuente broke between Hartley and Yarde, the conversion by Sánchez had the teams locked again at 25-all.

But although a series of big tackles by the Pumas brought roars from the crowd of just under 30,000, England were the team with the requisite strength and cohesion. In the 65th minute, Collier scored a catch-and-drive try after a punt by May had secured a good line-out position. Ford converted, and England stayed resolute through some niggly moments as May made a high tackle, Francis and Genge engaged in angry grapples, and Lavanini was lucky not to be shown a card for a blindsiding tackle that buckled Hughes's knee. With seven minutes remaining, Ford popped over a dropped goal from the ten-metre line to give England a ten-point lead. This they preserved as, first, two replacements, Matt Mullan and Wilson, held up the substitute Argentina scrum half Gonzalo Bertranou, and then a magnificently unmoving pack kept the Pumas out at a five-metre scrum.

Jones was inwardly delighted while he expressed several caveats with one eye on meeting Argentina again at the 2019 World Cup. 'A few guys have done really well,' the coach said. 'Harry Williams, Charlie Ewels, Tom Curry and Sam Underhill at open-side flanker, and Mark Wilson has proved himself to be a very competent player.

'[But] to beat Argentina at the World Cup, we are going to have to improve. They have edged us in certain departments and at the World Cup we will need a gap. Our next challenge is to go through our next phase undefeated. If we do that we go to the World Cup as number one, and that would give us reasons to be confident.'

SCOTLAND IN SINGAPORE, AUSTRALIA AND FIJI

by **ALAN LORIMER**

Alex Dunbar, operating in the mode of a flanker, forced Australia to concede a penalty at the ruck. It was all over. Scotland had achieved a historic victory, their first ever win against Australia in Sydney

Scotland's 2017 summer tour marked the beginning of Gregor Townsend's tenure in charge of the national team, and over three Tests against Italy, Australia and Fiji, it came close to producing the perfect start for the former international fly half. The Scots sweated it out in steamy Singapore for victory over Italy, hit a high with even sweeter success in Sydney against Australia, but were solidly sunk in Suva by Fiji, denying Townsend a three-Test clean sweep on his debut tour as head coach. Still, Scotland's

first ever win against Australia in Sydney was in itself enough to make three weeks of extensive travelling and exposure to some alien climates all worth it. Vern Cotter, Scotland's outgoing coach, had laid the basis for a more successful era, culminating in encouraging results from the 2016 autumn series of Tests and then a fourth-place finish, equal on points with Ireland and France, in the 2017 Six Nations. Townsend wanted to bring his style of rugby to the Scotland squad and the summer tour provided the ideal laboratory conditions.

Like the other home nations, Scotland had several top players on Lions duty, albeit there were only three Scots in Warren Gatland's squad. Additionally a number of players were still recovering from long-term injury, among them centre Huw Jones and prop Alasdair Dickinson. Moreover, from Townsend's original tour selection, lock Richie Gray, wing Sean Maitland and scrum half Sam Hidalgo-Clyne were late withdrawals. In the circumstances Townsend was presented with the opportunity to look at players hitherto untested at international level and several who had been discarded during the Vern Cotter reign. Among the new boys included was the Glasgow centre Nick Grigg while among the previously capped players brought back into the Scotland fold were the Edinburgh lock Ben Toolis and the Glasgow wing Lee Jones.

The notion of playing a Test match against Italy in Singapore had its critics but there was method in this particular tropical madness. Singapore's climate, it was argued, would come close to simulating what might be expected in Japan for the 2019 World Cup. In the event it was certainly a challenge for Scotland players emerging from cool May conditions back home to temperatures some 15 degrees higher in Singapore.

Scotland had reason to feel confident going into what was the first ever Tier One match played in

Singapore, having comfortably defeated the Azzurri at Murrayfield three months earlier in their final Six Nations match. Justification for this residual confidence came as Scotland, with fly half Finn Russell delivering an inspired performance, ran in five tries for a 34-13 victory.

Scrum half Ali Price showed his sharpness with a try on the blind side before Tim Visser converted a delicate infield kick by Russell for the Scots' second try. After the break Ross Ford finished off a trundling maul, and the hooker made it a brace after Russell showed handling skills of the highest order in the build-up to the score. Scotland's other try was scored by recalled wing Damien Hoyland, while for Italy the Exeter Chiefs centre Michele Campagnaro and wing Angelo Esposito scored late tries; not enough, however, to threaten the outcome.

The next stop for the Scots was Sydney and with it welcome relief from the heat and humidity of Singapore, and the chance to enjoy an Australian winter climate perfect for rugby. Scotland's two most recent matches against Australia, the 2015 Rugby World Cup quarter-final match and the 2016 autumn Test at Murrayfield had each resulted in a one-point winning margin for the Wallabies. The incentive therefore to achieve victory against Australia could not have been greater. In particular, what was seen as a faulty and match-deciding refereeing decision in the 2015 Rugby World Cup that resulted in Australia kicking the winning penalty goal just before full-time still rankled. Now was the chance for the Scots to right this 'wrong'.

Townsend rang the changes for the Test against Australia, the most significant of these being the repositioning of Duncan Taylor from full back to centre. Fittingly Ben Toolis, Brisbane-raised but qualified to play for Scotland through his mother, retained his place at lock to face the land of his birth.

Scotland had worked hard on their defence in the lead-up to the Sydney Test match and it paid off as early harassment of a much vaunted Wallabies side allowed Taylor to intercept a Will Genia pass and then romp in under the posts, leaving Russell with the simplest of conversions. Genia was again culpable when his attempted clearance kick was charged down by Russell, the Scotland fly half collecting the ball to score and then convert his side's second try.

The Scots had opened with a monster penalty kick from London Irish full back Greig Tonks; Australia, meanwhile, had missed a kick at goal by Bernard Foley. But three tries, two from their world-class full back Israel Folau – the first from defence-opening passing by Genia and Foley and the second from an accurate cross-kick by the Wallaby fly half – and the third a five-pointer from Genia, put Australia into a 19-17 lead.

An Australian radio commentator was heard to remark something along the lines of the Wallabies being the creative side and Scotland a disruptive team. The microphone was still crackling with these words when the Scots produced the try of the Test and indeed of the tour. It started with an audacious move just outside the Scotland 22-metre area. Three phases later after play that bore the Townsend stamp, the ball was spun wide to Lee Jones. The Glasgow wing wrong-footed two opponents then leapt over two defenders before linking with Taylor, who found flanker Hamish Watson on his inside to take the scoring pass.

> **BELOW** Tim Visser strikes for Scotland's second try in their 34-13 victory over Italy in Singapore on the first leg of their tour.
>
> **FACING PAGE** Scotland No. 8 Josh Strauss, supported by Hamish Watson, runs into Fiji's Joeli Veitayaki in Suva.
>
> **PAGES 66-67** Wayne Barnes signals a penalty against Australia in the last minute in Sydney and Scotland can start celebrating.

Russell converted for a 24-19 Scotland lead but the game was not yet over. In a final ten minutes of relentless Wallaby pressure the Scots defended heroically, their final statement of intent coming on the stroke of full-time when Alex Dunbar, operating in the mode of a flanker, forced Australia to concede a penalty at the ruck. It was all over. Scotland had achieved a historic victory, their first ever win against Australia in Sydney.

Within minutes of the final whistle the announcement came through that Russell and prop Allan Dell were to join the Lions squad. A further shrinking of the squad followed when Townsend revealed that Dunbar and flanker Magnus Bradbury were to return home as part of a pre-tour player welfare plan.

After the high of Sydney and with gaps in the squad it was always going to be difficult for the Scots to face Fiji in the tropical conditions of Suva. Townsend, very much a fan of Fijian rugby, had reason to be wary of playing the Fijians on their home soil, having been a member of the Scotland 1998 team that lost 51-26 in Suva when the great Waisale Serevi, who had dazzled on the World Sevens stage, showed he was equally devastating in the Fifteens game. Townsend, now with four players fewer in his squad, selected several as yet unused tour members. Ruaridh Jackson, Nick Grigg and Alex Allan made their first appearances of the tour while Henry Pyrgos and Tim Swinson were given first starts.

Fiji, with Rugby World Cup qualifying matches in mind, had assembled a strong squad that contained Europe-based players, among them the Racing 92 lock and Olympic gold medallist Leone Nakarawa, a cult hero at Scotstoun during his three-year stint with Glasgow Warriors. Nakarawa is best remembered at Glasgow for his performance against Munster in the PRO12 final at Kingspan when his athletic running and his outrageous offloading made him the star of the show. Against a Scotland side struggling in the enervating conditions of Suva, it was these Nakarawa skills that opened the Scots' defence for Fiji to score their two tries, by flanker Peceli Yato and replacement scrum half Henry Seniloli.

Further damage was done by the goal-kicking of fly half Ben Volavola who landed five penalty goals and a conversion in Fiji's 27-22 win. By contrast the Scots eschewed opportunities to punish Fijian indiscipline with kicks at goal, opting more often to go for the corner. That worked twice, resulting in driving-maul tries for Ross Ford, who became the most capped Scottish player on his 110th appearance for the national side, and Fraser Brown. A third try for Scotland was scored by Ruaridh Jackson after the ball had squirted out of a ruck, the Harlequins player further contributing with two conversions and a penalty goal. 'It's not the result we wanted. We didn't deserve to win. The tour was going well up to this point so it's very disappointing to slip up,' admitted the Scotland captain, John Barclay.

The defeat in Suva underlined Scotland's dependence on Finn Russell in the pivot role and the pointlessness of flying the Scottish playmaker to New Zealand and then making such scant use of him in the Lions game against the Hurricanes. Scottish rugby may now have depth in most positions but at fly half the stock is desperately low, a situation, however, that could provide prime opportunities for the likes of young players Connor Eastgate and Adam Hastings to step up to senior international level sooner than expected.

Overall the tour gave Townsend a clearer picture of who's who in the new pecking order. Undoubtedly two of the biggest gainers will be lock Ben Toolis and utility back Duncan Taylor, two quality players who fit into the Townsend style of play. Although defeat to Fiji in the final match was disappointing for Scotland, their victory over a full-strength Australia side gave Townsend and his squad a new self-belief to lift Scottish rugby out of what has been a difficult decade.

WALES IN THE PACIFIC

by GRAHAM CLUTTON

With all the focus on the British & Irish Lions and their hotly anticipated series with New Zealand, Wales had already lost three coaches and 12 of their best players to the meetings with the All Blacks

If ever a national side succeeded in the face of adversity, this was it. Wales, under the guidance of coach Robin McBryde, travelled to the southern hemisphere with their two-Test summer tour of Tonga and Samoa ravaged by problems before they had even left the team's domestic base in the Vale of Glamorgan. With all the focus on the British & Irish Lions and their hotly anticipated series with New Zealand, Wales had already lost three coaches and 12 of their best players to the meetings with the All Blacks. Head coach Warren Gatland was once again in charge of the Lions, and Rob Howley and Neil Jenkins were among his back-room team, leaving McBryde to lead the party against two of the Pacific Island nations.

The former hooker didn't have the greatest of starts either. He saw Cardiff Blues coach Danny Wilson and Scarlets backs coach Stephen Jones – both of whom had been due to join the Wales set-up – pull out in the weeks prior to departure, citing regional commitments. Furthermore, with safety concerns over the playing facilities in Tonga, it was decided at the eleventh hour that the opening game of the tour would be played in Auckland.

Without the likes of Sam Warburton, Alun Wyn Jones and George North, McBryde's 32-man party had an understandably youthful look. A total of 13 uncapped players were named in a squad captained by the experienced centre Jamie Roberts. After being dropped for the first time in his Wales career following a poor display against Australia the previous November, Roberts was a surprise choice to lead McBryde's men. Fellow midfielder Scott Williams had been favourite to be named skipper, but Roberts' enthusiasm for taking charge of one of the youngest Wales squads in recent history shone through.

'I wanted the young lads who came in to have the time of their lives playing for their country,' said Roberts, who narrowly missed out on what would have been his third Lions tour.

'It's a hugely privileged position to play rugby for Wales. It's every boy's dream. I wanted the guys to have the most fun possible. I truly believe you do your best work when you enjoy what you do.

'The challenge for Welsh rugby has always been the strength in depth behind the first-choice 23. Tours like the one we went on are so crucial to develop players because come the 2019 World Cup, we are going to need 35 to 40 players who are ready to do a job at the highest level.'

McBryde's decision to leave out flanker James Davies – who had been in outstanding form for the Scarlets in their unlikely but thoroughly deserved Guinness PRO12 title triumph – was the one surprise from the squad announcement. However, fresh faces Keelan Giles, Steffan Evans and Ollie Griffiths meant Wales departed for New Zealand on 8 June piled high with youthful exuberance.

McBryde himself was a late arrival at Wales's base in Takapuna on the outskirts of Auckland – his wife had a heart scare in the days prior to departure – but with a full week to prepare before facing Tonga, the tourists quickly shook off the challenges of jet lag and set to work.

Of the 13 new faces in the squad, nine were picked to face Tonga. The headline selection was 21-year-old second-row Seb Davies – who had just a handful of games of senior rugby to his name with Cardiff Blues prior to being picked by McBryde. Wing Evans and Wasps flanker Thomas Young were also selected to start a Test match for the first time, with six international rookies in Ryan Elias, Wyn Jones, Dillon Lewis, Griffiths, Aled Davies and Owen Williams among the replacements.

Sam Davies, who had impressed off the bench in the Six Nations, began a Test match for the first time as well, at outside half. If inexperience had been an understandable worry for Wales, it didn't materialise on the field as McBryde's side sealed a fully deserved 24-6 victory over a plucky yet limited Tonga. The game

was a curtain-raiser for the All Blacks' 78-0 thrashing of Samoa, and Wales could and should have won by more, Sam Davies missing with three kicks at goal. Ultimately, Alex Cuthbert's impressive score – created by full back Gareth Anscombe – and a late penalty try were enough for Wales to open their tour with a victory. Sam Davies ended the game with 12 points, and he, his namesake Seb and Anscombe were the stand-out performers, while the only downside for McBryde was a shoulder injury to Cuthbert which would rule him out of the game against Samoa.

'The conditions were tough with the rain that came down in the second half. We blew a couple of opportunities and could have put the game to bed in the first half,' said Sam Davies. 'But fair play to Tonga, they didn't go away.

'We fronted up in defence and controlled the game in the second half and that's credit to the boys. I missed some kicks I should have got, but it's all about bouncing back and I was able to do that. I stuck to my process, stayed calm, and struck a couple of important kicks in the second half. I had to make sure I nailed them and I did.'

With a win under their belt, Wales headed for Samoa without Cuthbert and four other senior players in Kristian Dacey, Tomas Francis, Cory Hill and Gareth Davies. The quartet were controversially called up to the Lions squad and were joined by Scotland duo Allan Dell and Finn Russell to become the so-called 'Geography Six'.

The decision to summon them was based on their proximity to New Zealand and while they failed to make an appearance for Gatland's side, their departure was a further blow to a Wales outfit already stretched to its limits. It meant that as he arrived in the sweltering heat of the Samoan capital Apia, McBryde was forced to shuffle the deck further. For what was always going to be the tougher Test of the tour, in came Aled Davies at scrum half, prop Lewis, hooker Elias and lock Rory Thornton. In total, Wales's starting team contained just 151 caps of international experience and 92 of those belonged to Roberts.

BELOW Wales stand-off Sam Davies takes a shot at goal against Tonga at Eden Park, Auckland, watched by namesake Seb.

FACING PAGE Scrum half Aled Davies, in his first start for Wales, launches the ball upfield against Samoa in Apia.

PAGES 70-71 Gareth Anscombe gives Viliami Tahitu'a the slip in the driving rain as Wales beat Tonga 24-6.

In alien territory and up against a Samoan side who had beaten them in their last meeting in 2012, Wales were underdogs. Somehow, though, they defied logic and even a brutal sickness bug to seal a 19-17 success in appalling conditions.

In the week building up to the game, the Wales camp suffered with severe vomiting and diarrhoea, and skipper Roberts was one of a handful of players ill at half-time at Apia Park. It made the win – which was achieved thanks to Evans' first two international tries – all the more impressive.

The match was played on a poor surface which cut up following torrential rain – conditions that suited Samoa's huge pack down to the ground. But a young Wales eight matched the Pacific Islanders up front and Sam Davies' three first-half penalties kept his team in the game at the break.

In the second half Evans stamped his mark on the international scene. His first try might have been a simple finish, but his second was a superb effort in the corner and proved to be the game's vital moment. It meant that against all the odds, Wales returned home with a 100 per cent record and safe in the knowledge they have young players coming through to help challenge for the 2019 World Cup.

Seb Davies, Sam Davies and Evans all shone, while more senior figures Roberts and Anscombe impressed in leadership roles. It left coach and captain delighted at what they had seen.

'It was a very difficult tour in such a short space of time. Tonga in Auckland was tough and you can't underestimate the situation we had to deal with in Samoa,' McBryde said.

'Conditions were poor for both teams and we had illness in the camp. The boys could have used that as an excuse, but they dug in so deep. I'm just so pleased for the players.'

Roberts added: 'To tour Tonga and Samoa was a great opportunity for the players; I doubt they'll get to play there again for Wales.

'It's not like touring New Zealand, South Africa or Australia. It was a once in a career opportunity.

'To captain Wales was a huge honour for me and probably one of my proudest moments. To see the smiles on the faces of the young boys was brilliant.

'The boys played for each other and the jersey and you can't ask for much more than that. I'm sure the magnitude of what they achieved will sink in in years to come.'

IRELAND IN THE USA AND JAPAN

by **PETER O'REILLY**

Setting out, only nine of the 32-man squad had caps in double figures, and eight were uncapped. All eight saw action and everyone involved will have benefited from spending the guts of a month in camp

No book will be written about Ireland's summer tour of 2017 to the US and Japan. No film companies are currently squabbling over the movie rights. That it happened at the same time as a British & Irish Lions tour, which itself featured 11 of Ireland's top players, helped to ensure that the tour would stay 'beneath the radar'. Throw in unsociable kick-off times for your home television audience and you're virtually guaranteed a degree of obscurity.

Realistically, the only way to make the news when you're playing three Tests against Tier Two opponents is to lose – as Wales did in Japan four years ago, coincidentally in a Lions season. But Ireland never looked remotely in danger of losing against the US Eagles in Harrison, New Jersey, and only in the second of two Tests against the Brave Blossoms, in Tokyo, were they truly, albeit briefly, discommoded. A try count of 21-8 in favour of Ireland over three Tests illustrates the supremacy of Joe Schmidt's largely experimental squad.

For all that, this was an important venture as the first step on the road to the 2019 World Cup, which just happens to be in Japan, whose national team just happens to be in Ireland's pool. The second two weeks gave players critical insights into conditions, facilities, culture and of course opposition. And it gave Schmidt a better picture about who is best equipped to be part of a World Cup squad.

His plans are coloured by his memories of the last tournament, in the UK in 2015, when his lack of depth in certain positions was ruthlessly exposed by Argentina in the quarter-finals. From that point on, the Kiwi's medium-term strategy has been about building a 30/31-man squad, all of whom can add value, rather than just take up a space on a plane.

Some of these kids will be around for the World Cup after next, in 2023, which Ireland hopes to host. The IRFU's vote-gathering process is already well under way and one of the main reasons for playing a Test in the US en route to Japan was surely because it allowed the union the opportunity to win friends and to influence. Why else would Ireland begin a tour to the Far East by flying west? Rarely can Ireland have covered so many air miles on a summer tour.

But there were no complaints from the coach. Every hour of teacher-pupil contact at this time of year, when there are no provincial distractions, is time well spent. Schmidt was happy to take a punt on certain youngsters, given that he had a core of experience in the pack, where Cian Healy, Devin Toner and Rhys Ruddock started every game, plus the class and experience out wide of Keith Earls, who was splendidly sharp from start to finish. Setting out, only nine of the 32-man squad had caps in double figures, and eight were uncapped – Dave Heffernan, Rory Scannell, Kieran Treadwell, Rory O'Loughlin, John Cooney, James Ryan, Andrew Porter and Jacob Stockdale – and the last three in that list were part of the Irish Under 20 side the previous season. All eight saw action and everyone involved will have benefited from spending the guts of a month in camp.

Who benefited most? Jack Conan is the name which springs most readily to mind. It's nearly two years since the Leinster No. 8 made his Ireland debut, in a World Cup warm-up against Scotland at the Aviva Stadium, and for much of the intervening period he was frustrated by either injury or lack of opportunity. Here, he started every Test, all of them in trying climatic conditions – more trying than they will be at an autumn World Cup – and missed only four minutes of action in total. His pace and power allowed him to

ABOVE No. 8 Jack Conan runs in Ireland's fourth try of the first Test against Japan in Shizuoka, which the tourists won 50-22.

FACING PAGE Jacob Stockdale, a try scorer in this his debut Test, tangles with USA No. 8 Dave Tameilau in New Jersey.

PAGES 76-77 Tour skipper Rhys Ruddock offloads to debutant John Cooney during the second Test against Japan in Tokyo.

win collisions consistently, and he now offers both Leinster and Ireland a decent No. 8 alternative to 33-year-old Jamie Heaslip.

Second-row depth is now less of concern for Schmidt, too. At his squad announcement, the coach faced a lengthy interrogation about the absence of Racing 92-bound Donnacha Ryan, who'd had such an excellent Six Nations campaign. Happily, two new locks emerged from the tour with credit. Twenty-one-year-old Ulster second-row Kieran Treadwell made his debut off the bench in Shizuoka and showed enough dynamism and industry to earn a start the following week in Tokyo. Perhaps an even bigger success, however, was 20-year-old James Ryan, who joined that exclusive band of players – Brian O'Driscoll is its best-known member – who have been capped at senior level by their country before their province. He scored with his very first touch in New Jersey and never looked less than a special talent.

Jacob Stockwell was the pick of the new backs. He offers size and versatility – quick enough to play on the wing, where he scored on debut against the Eagles, but also a sound footballer and secure enough under the high ball to thrive at full back, as he showed in the same game. It will be interesting to see how Ulster use him, given they are so well stocked in the back three. Ireland's most potent outside back on this tour, however, was Keith Earls, who scored four tries, making him the first Irish player to score nine tries in an international season. In carrying for a whopping 370 metres over the course of three games, he also provided a handful of assists. The 29-year-old could not have expressed more eloquently his determination to overcome the disappointment of missing out on Lions selection.

Earls dominated the New Jersey Test, a nine-tries-to-three romp in which the only serious discomfort for the tourists was the humidity. The only Irish player who struggled was Joey Carbery. The Leinster player came on tour on the back of a spectacular season, in which he made his Test debut in the victory over New Zealand in Chicago and then dazzled in a Champions Cup quarter-final victory over Wasps. Here, he went into the Test boosted by some warm praise from Ronan O'Gara, one of three young coaches who spent time with Schmidt on tour – Girvan Dempsey and Felix Jones took turns for the Japanese leg. But the game was something of a disaster for the 21-year-old, as two Eagles tries came as a direct result of his errors. To compound matters, Carbery injured his ankle and played no further part in the tour. If there's any sort of blessing, it's that his first major setback should happen now, rather than in the Six Nations or at a World Cup. He'll be stronger mentally for the experience.

Rugby's growing popularity in Japan was clear the following week when over 27,000 fans turned up at the first Test in Shizuoka. Unfortunately, they witnessed no giant-killing in the manner of the famous victory over South Africa in Brighton at the last World Cup. Jamie Joseph's team was hammered 50-22 by an Irish side showing six changes from New Jersey. One of those, Leinster's Dan Leavy, celebrated by scoring a couple of tries and impressing with his energy levels in sweltering conditions. His old St Michael's schoolmate Luke McGrath also made the most of his opportunity at scrum half.

Schmidt surely yearned for a meaningful challenge, though. He got it in Tokyo seven days later, before a crowd of just under 30,000 at the Ajinomoto Stadium. The 35-13 scoreline suggests a relatively facile victory but Japan rallied well from half-time to match Ireland with a try apiece in a torrid second half, in which the coach needed to make full use of his bench.

'Some guys have really put their foot forward and other guys clearly have a bit more work to do,' Schmidt said afterwards, when asked about the usefulness of the tour as a whole. 'It's given us clarity around that.

'Rhys Ruddock did a fantastic job leading on the pitch but away from the pitch as well. It's important to learn stuff like that. The depth of players is important but you also need depth of character. He really brought that to the job. Keith Earls is another guy who has led on and off the pitch. He's been sensational.

'I'd like to think we are building depth. We are open-minded about it. Every bracket of games we have played recently, new players have emerged. Last Six Nations it was Josh van der Flier. Garry Ringrose came in last November and has become a regular member of the team. Right at the end of this Six Nations Andrew Conway came in and played his first 40 minutes of Test footie.'

The experience of playing two games in Japan is something Schmidt believes will be an advantage when Ireland return in two years for the World Cup. '[It's good] just getting to know the differences in culture, some of the expectations around what you have to do off the pitch as much as anything,' he said. 'Timing yourself to get to training venues – it's taking 45 minutes. We are used to walking from the door, down the road and straight on the pitch. We allowed 70 minutes to arrive here on a bus to the Ajinomoto Stadium. You don't ideally want to be travelling 70 minutes but that may be the fact of it when it comes to World Cup time.'

The word is that the hosts are planning not to use the pool game against Ireland as the tournament opener, mainly because they believe they have a better chance of causing an upset if they face Scotland in that match and leave the Ireland encounter until game three. Whatever happens, Schmidt is bound to be better informed and well armed on the strength of this venture.

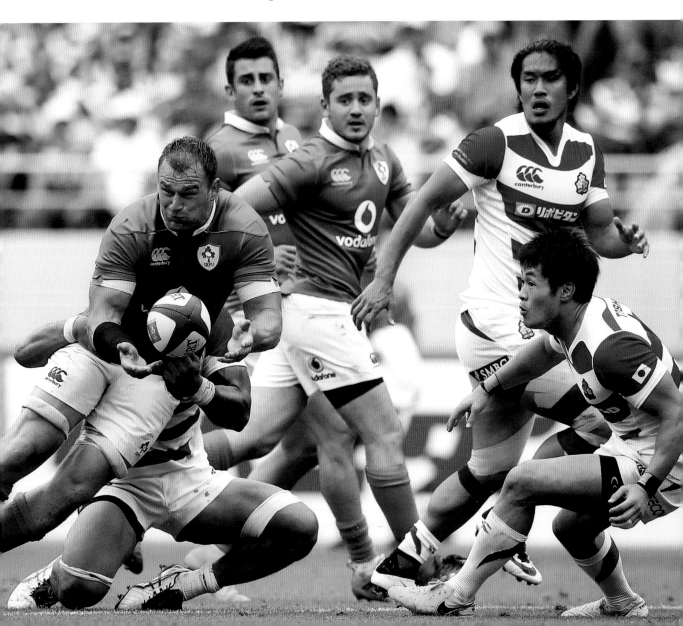

next

ARE HAPPY TO SUPPORT

THE WOODEN SPOON

3
HOME
FRONT

A Family Affair
RUGBY FATHERS AND SONS

by **CHRIS JONES**

The Youngs, Robinsons, Fords and Farrells are part of an unusual dynamic in English professional rugby which also includes Jim Mallinder, the Northampton director of rugby, and his son Harry

I t should have been the perfect end to a tumultuous season for the Young family: Dai leads Wasps to the Aviva Premiership title, with son Thomas a key figure in the victory over Exeter at Twickenham in the play-off final before heading off on tour with Wales.

However, father and son stories in rugby rarely produce fairy tales as the Youngs can testify. While Wasps suffered extra-time agony as they lost 23-20 to Exeter, the Young family could still look back with pride on an amazing season during which rugby's father and son relationships suffered highs and desperate lows.

The raw emotion flanker Olly Robinson expressed when his father Andy was sacked as Bristol director of rugby earlier in the season revealed just how complicated rugby life can become. Knowing his father had been shown the door, Robinson junior had to get on with his career as a key member of the struggling Bristol side that failed to avoid relegation.

George Ford was so deeply hurt by father Mike's removal as Bath director of rugby that staying with the club became impossible to accept and he moved to Leicester at the end of the season. Owen Farrell, Ford's schoolboy friend, had already been forced to come to terms with father Andy's departure from the England coaching set-up; he is now Ireland's defence coach, with the rest of the family having moved from Hertfordshire to Dublin. The pair were reunited on the Lions tour to New Zealand, with Andy

LEFT Owen Farrell (player) and father Andy Farrell (assistant coach) chat in Auckland during the 2017 Lions tour of New Zealand.

FACING PAGE George Ford (player) and father Mike Ford (director of rugby), both then at Bath, at the Aviva Premiership Rugby Awards in May 2015.

having travelled to Edinburgh to cheer on Owen as he helped Saracens retain the European Champions Cup with victory over Clermont.

The Youngs, Robinsons, Fords and Farrells are part of an unusual dynamic in English professional rugby which also includes Jim Mallinder, the Northampton director of rugby, and his son Harry, who is in his first-team squad and was taken to Argentina with England in the summer. As the Youngs, Robinsons, Fords and Farrells can testify, the delicate balance that has to be found in these situations can be suddenly disrupted with dramatic effect on the families involved. There is the unconfined joy of seeing your son develop from mini-rugby into the senior sport, but how do you avoid accusations of bias when a dad is suddenly employing his own son?

It is not as simple as saying that rugby can be left outside when father and son return to the family home. Life isn't that black and white, which makes Ford's decision to quit Bath understandable because he still carries the hurt of seeing his father dumped by the owners. Robinson has been very open about the 'anger' he feels at the way Bristol treated his father, who watched from the stands during the rest of the season because he wanted to show support for his lad.

For Dai Young, what has happened to other rugby families is painfully familiar following his move from the Blues to Wasps and he knows the Youngs may have to go through hard times again in the future. Young is convinced that Thomas was forced out of the Blues, having come through the club's academy, because he

was his son. Young understood the rationale at the time, but that didn't lessen the belief he was solely responsible for his son's situation.

Young explained: 'Thomas hasn't done it the easy way and has had many obstacles to overcome and I am probably the biggest. What I mean by that is Thomas came through all the age groups and just as he came up to the Blues, I moved on. I had been there eight or nine years and when I left the first thing the new person coming in does is dismantle that, to put their own stamp on things. Pretty much it was a case of the coach not wanting him there because he was my son.

'It is a difficult relationship but he is always going to be my son and Mike Ford, Andy Farrell, Jim Mallinder and Andy Robinson understand the situation. You do try not to treat them any differently and Thomas doesn't get any favours in selection.

'Coming here, Thomas had to fight and I am very proud of him because he has done it the tough way and no one handed him anything. With all of the back-row talent we have here, he has had to fight for his opportunities and has taken them. He deserves all the plaudits that have come his way. He has worked really hard having to double prove himself because people are only human and will say "he's only there because of his father". It comes with the territory.'

The success of both Youngs has raised the possibility of both moving on at some point, with dad one of the favourites to replace Warren Gatland and Thomas' inclusion in the Wales squad making him a hot rugby property. Young senior also knows, as the Ford, Robinson and Farrell stories have shown, rugby life can be turned upside down at any moment. Young added: 'I hope that if I get sacked tomorrow that Thomas would be a bit upset and I am sure if he came in and said he wanted to go to Leicester I would be a bit upset!'

It is now the turn of the Mallinder and Young sons to face suggestions that their fathers are either being too hard or giving them preferential treatment at their clubs. Thomas has been told by other Wasps players his dad does give him a much tougher time in training although he insists this doesn't really enter the equation. 'On occasions people at the club say he is a bit harder on me than he would be on others, but I wouldn't want it any other way,' said the 25-year-old open-side flanker, who is one of three rugby-playing brothers.

'Things weren't going that well for me and then he gave me the opportunity to come to Wasps and every time I take the pitch I want to repay him for giving me the chance. I didn't have much to do with Dad at the Blues but at Wasps I know that as soon as I walk into the building each day it's work and he is the boss. When we get home it reverts back to a normal father and son relationship. My brothers came up for the Bath game and the whole family then travelled home to Wales on Christmas morning then it was back for training the next day.'

Dai and Thomas watch rugby together in the family home and while they discuss other teams, it never strays into Wasps talk. That stays outside the front door and appears to be a non-negotiable part of making a father and son scenario work for everyone in the family. 'We can have a sit-down and watch a game and we talk about a good tackle or a clear-out at a ruck,' said Young senior. 'It doesn't then go into we should be doing this or that at Wasps. The reality is that when he is at home you try and get back into the father-son relationship and I cannot divorce myself from that, and when he is at Wasps training can I forget he is my son? No, I can't because he is always going to be my son and it will always be slightly difficult and of course I may be a bit harder on him.

'I am proud of my three sons and one of them just happens to be playing here at Wasps. My other sons are at Aberdare RFC and have a bit of brains because they don't play in the front row. Lewis is a No. 8 and Owen is No. 7 and so we have two of those – either my wife is really quick or the milkman.'

BELOW Flanker Thomas Young, capped by Wales on the 2017 summer tour, in action for Wasps against Saracens in the Premiership.

FACING PAGE Dai Young (left), Thomas's father and his director of rugby at Wasps, in the front row for Wales against England in 2001.

On the Up
THE RISE OF HARTPURY COLLEGE

by **NEALE HARVEY**

Hartpury have so far produced over 150 male and female players who have gone on to play international rugby, whether that be at age-group level or in the Test arena like Moriarty, May, Genge and Cuthbert

In September 2004, newly formed Hartpury College set out on their first season in lowly Gloucestershire Three North – Level 11 of the English rugby union pyramid and about as far removed from the glamorous elite end of the professional game as one could imagine.

Trips to Gloucester All Blues, Tredworth and Newent would hardly send pulses racing but little though they knew it at the time, the pioneering students of Hartpury were about to pave the way for a rise through the league system that has been nothing short of spectacular.

Promotion at the end of that 2004-05 season heralded the first of seven successive league title wins – a run that saw them reach National League Two (Level 4) in express time after losing just four of 148 matches. Their success did not gain universal approval from more traditional local clubs who believed Hartpury's lavish, partly taxpayer-funded facilities provided an unfair advantage, but games still needed to be won and the college's desire to develop players had paid off.

Not that Hartpury's journey would stop there. Fuelled by the ambition of then director of rugby Alan Martinovic, whose background as a driving force behind the highly successful player production line at the renowned Colston's School in Bristol led Hartpury to recruit him in 2009, Gloucestershire's premier students outfit consolidated in National Two before moving up again in 2014 and setting out on another three-year charge to reach the Championship.

A ninth promotion in 13 seasons was duly achieved last April. Not only that, Hartpury went through the card undefeated, claiming 148 of the 150 match points available, scoring 1455 points and setting a standard that had not been seen in National League rugby since a heavily funded Northampton side laid waste to all-comers during their single season in the second tier following relegation from the Premiership in 2007 – a truly staggering achievement.

What really stands out about Hartpury, though, are the players produced by the college who have gone on to bigger and better things. Amongst recent alumni to make it to the top are Gloucester and British & Irish Lions back-rower Ross Moriarty, Gloucester and England wing Jonny May, Leicester and England prop Ellis Genge and Cardiff and Wales flyer Alex Cuthbert. Dan Robson (Wasps), Billy Burns and Tom Savage (both Gloucester) and Ryan Mills (Worcester) are amongst a host of current Premiership stars to have played for Hartpury, while of last season's all-conquering National One squad, captain Seb Negri (Treviso), winger Jonas Mikalcius (Harlequins) and back-rower Jake Polledri (Gloucester) are now moving into top-flight rugby.

Martinovic, one of the architects of this success along with his predecessor Allan Lewis, departed for Bristol last year, but current director of rugby John Barnes, who arrived at Hartpury in 2010 after serving Bristol for ten years as a coach, believes the influence of college rugby in producing elite-standard players will keep growing.

BELOW Jonas Mikalcius in full flight for Hartpury RFC. The wing, who hails from Lithuania, is on the books at Harlequins.

FACING PAGE Hartpury old boy Ross Moriarty, here in action for the club in 2013-14, is now a Wales international and a Lion.

As well as claiming the National League One title, Hartpury were inaugural winners of the new British Universities & Colleges Sport (BUCS) Super Rugby championship and then doubled up by winning the competition's knockout cup.

'College rugby is certainly on the up,' says Barnes. 'Academy players now are encouraged to study alongside their playing commitments and for those who don't make it in the professional game or get injured and are released, it means more players are heading to college teams. We've seen that this year with the people applying to join us and last year BUCS rugby saw some top-quality players playing high-quality rugby week in, week out. There's been some good financial backing from the RFU, so combined with tough National League rugby it's producing very good players.

'Loughborough have been strong for a number of years now and were with us in National One, while Exeter University are climbing the league system fast and have a great link with Exeter Chiefs, the new Premiership champions. Bath, Leeds Beckett, Northumbria and Durham all have good rugby programmes and this season we'll see Nottingham Trent join BUCS Super Rugby. They have a very close relationship with Nottingham Rugby in the Championship so they'll be another strong addition and will only get better. With the added competition and a good geographical spread, college rugby is growing and that can only be of huge benefit to English rugby. The only disappointment is that none of the London universities or colleges seem to be challenging any more.'

Hartpury have so far produced over 150 male and female players who have gone on to play international rugby, whether that be at age-group level or in the Test arena like Moriarty, May, Genge and Cuthbert. Barnes added: 'It was great to see Ross Moriarty on the Lions tour, albeit he had to come home early, and the more players we see like him, May and Genge playing at the highest level of the game, the better it is for Hartpury College. You'd hope that over the next five years, with us now being in the Championship, more will go on to gain representative honours.

'Player development is what Hartpury is all about and that's credit to the vision and the rugby programmes devised by people like Allan Lewis and Alan Martinovic. Alan Martinovic changed things massively so that our rugby programme encompassed the 16-18 age group, which over the last seven or eight years has been so successful. He created a pathway for players to come in at 16 and continue into higher

education while pursuing their rugby ambitions, so hopefully we'll now see guys like Seb Negri, Jonas Mikalcius and Jake Polledri fulfil their Test potential.

'I'm fortunate to be in charge now when we're at the highest level of league and BUCS rugby we've ever been, but Allan Lewis and Alan Martinovic were highly influential for me and I'm just looking to carry on that success. We're BUCS champions and cup winners and we're aspiring to be so again this season. It'll be quite difficult balancing our midweek BUCS commitments with competing in the Championship at weekends, but we've got a decent-sized squad who train together quite a lot so it's a pretty seamless transition from BUCS up to the side that plays weekends.'

From such humble beginnings in the Gloucestershire leagues, Hartpury now find themselves competing against the financial might of Bristol, Ealing and Jersey, as well as established Championship sides like Bedford, Cornish Pirates and Nottingham. On paper it looks a Herculean task, but Hartpury have recruited 12 new players, some of whom have Premiership and Championship experience, and Barnes is encouraged by the exploits of Richmond, who remained part-time after being promoted to the Championship last year but survived. Barnes explained: 'It's going to be difficult and some teams will be quite a bit stronger than us with the financial resources they've got. Despite having a successful season last year people will still see us as a target, but we're hopefully well prepared for it and we can take encouragement from what Richmond did last season. They stayed part-time, recruited very astutely and performed really well to finish above Rotherham. Once they got their first win they showed they could really compete by beating the likes of London Scottish, Bedford, Cornish Pirates and Nottingham.'

Hartpury will not be breaking the bank, with Barnes adding: 'We've brought in 12 players, a few of whom are ex-Hartpury guys anyway, and the majority will study here. As soon as we got promoted last season we had agents all over us trying to sell us players, but they don't understand that we're going to stay part-time and adhere to our ethos of being a college team. There's no point in us not giving students the opportunity to play in whatever level we're at on a Saturday; we want to provide the best standard for students to play in and that is always our driving force.'

BELOW The all-conquering Hartpury RFC squad and staff of 2016-17. The club played 30 and won 30 in National League One.

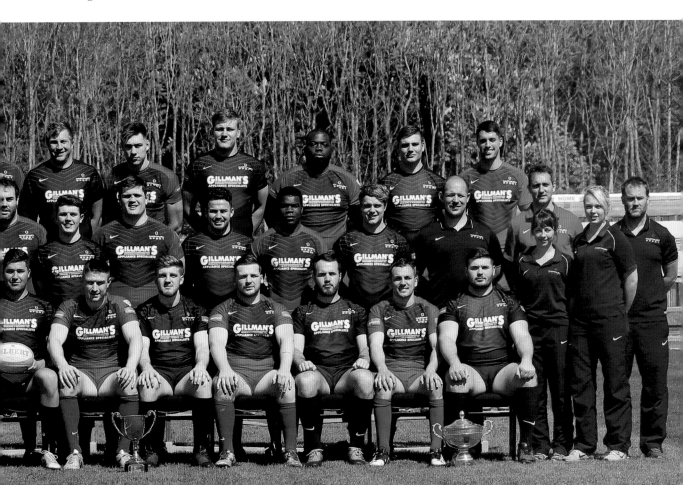

Arbuthnot Latham
is proud to support
Wooden Spoon
Rugby World

Fit for Purpose?
PERCEPTIONS OF THE PRO12

by **STEVE BALE**

Since then the Irish have had six European Cup winners and three runners-up. On that basis, it is inaccurate and unfair for anyone in Wales to complain that the PRO12 does not do the job for them

If the Guinness PRO12 gets a regular panning out of keeping with the exalted rugby played by the Scarlets at its 2017 culmination, it is worth noting that the criticism tends mostly to come from the land of the champions. It worked perfectly for the Scarlets.

Whether the PRO12 is fit for purpose for Wales is a different topic from whether it is fit for purpose. Either way the question ignores the point that any league in rugby has to have a discrete life of its own that has nothing to do with the international game which, at one remove, it serves. This truism helps explain the strength of the English Premiership and French Top 14, but also the unending

BELOW Scarlets' Canada international wing DTH van der Merwe dives in to score his side's fifth try of the 2017 Guinness PRO12 final against Munster at the Aviva Stadium.

tension – even when there is détente – between these two splendid, big-money competitions and the England and France teams respectively. The PRO12 has less money and is more nuanced, partly because it is already multinational before even considering adding South African franchises, let alone one from Germany. In any case, there are not too many complaints from the Irish that it fails to serve their needs.

Much was made of the meritocracy for European qualification imposed when the Heineken Cup became the Champions Cup in 2014. But the reality is the Irish overwhelmingly dominated both the PRO12 and the PRO12's European contribution before and after the change. As much as anything, this has to do with 'alignment', a terrible cliché of a word, and loyalty. The four proud provinces of Ireland pre-existed professionalism as rugby teams as well as geographical entities so were there as names with affiliations to be exploited. But it still needed an Irish vision. Anyone who had occasion to attend, say, a Pontypool-Munster match as used to take place annually in the old days will recall that these were utterly low-key affairs of small significance. People in Pontypool were more likely to have heard of Garryowen or Shannon than the province.

The four Welsh 'regions', a non-existent concept all those years ago, are artificial constructs by comparison. The same might be said of Glasgow and Edinburgh as the boiled-down Scottish 'districts' have become. In the end in both countries it came down to affordability. But as the Scarlets dazzlingly showed last May – and Glasgow, for that matter, in 2015 – the Welsh and Scots do have it in them to make a proper championship challenge. The difference is that, when it happens, it becomes almost a thing of wonder.

In Ireland it is routine, even down to the distinctly non-routine achievement of Connacht in taking the title in 2016 – in an all-Irish final, mark you – the Cinderellas by becoming princesses meaning all four provinces had won this league in one year or another.

Thanks to the Scarlets, champions twice, and the Ospreys, four times, the Welsh record since the invention of the regions is actually quite good. These six titles compare with seven for the Irish and one for the Scots. The deadbeat Italians of course are nowhere. The difference is the Blues and the Dragons have made no contribution at all as prize winners. It is no wonder Wales – despite the more favourable figures for the neighbours in the West – wonders at the efficacy of the PRO12 when only two, not four, have ever had a hope.

Perhaps the 2016-17 season will have marked a change. Improvement at Cardiff Blues under Danny Wilson has taken place but is slow. Newport Gwent Dragons, now given some reason to believe by being bought out by the Welsh Rugby Union, contrived to finish below even Treviso. That takes some doing. By comparison, the Ospreys were up there with the leaders all season long, and playing decent rugby for two-thirds of it until a virtual collapse at the very moment they needed to keep going. A semi-final place was hardly a consolation.

The Scarlets did it the other way round, losing their first three fixtures before embarking on a run of 17 victories in 19 games that proved them just as capable as the Irish big beasts in Leinster and Munster of surviving both the autumn and the Six Nations depletions. That alone would be a tribute to Wayne Pivac's man management and far-sightedness. But equally pertinent was how Scarlets' Kiwi coach assembled a brilliant cast list on limited resources and carried on developing rugby of style and substance even after those early discouragements. So much so that even the regrettable loss of Liam Williams to Saracens, not to mention that of DTH van der Merwe to Newcastle, became manageable by those Williams left behind. Pivac's canny compatriot Hadleigh Parkes could not even make Scarlets' starting XV for either the semi-final or final.

In Jonathan Davies and Scott Williams, Pivac has a centre partnership at least as potent as the vaunted Robbie Henshaw-Garry Ringrose version at Leinster. At 22, Steffan Evans is already a wondrous wing; we can but imagine what he may become.

BELOW Steve Shingler dots down for Cardiff Blues against Newport Gwent Dragons. Neither region has ever won the PRO12 title.

FACING PAGE Connacht and Glasgow in action in the 2016-17 PRO12. Glasgow became the league's first Scottish winners in 2015; Connacht's success in 2016 meant all four Irish provinces had lifted the title.

But Pivac's PRO12 triumph extends far further. Johnny McNicholl, Rhys Patchell, Gareth Davies . . . none of them would do a thing if their coach had not assembled a pack of forwards capable of gaining, and giving them, attacking ball.

So, four Wales tight forwards supplemented in particular by the eccentric and nonconformist flanker James Davies. Jonathan's kid brother may sometimes behave like a kid to make his national selectors reluctant, but in both the semi-final and final he was spectacularly influential.

The depth of the Scarlets' original rut made his and their soaring climax giddier still, not merely beating but trouncing Leinster then Munster in Dublin. A brand of risk-taking rugby specifically written into the constitution of the Llanelli club from whom the Scarlets sprang.

It was also, by the way, rugby in accordance with a Welsh historical stereotype more or less forgotten in recent times, where astute, deep- and quick-thinking individuals compensated for supposed physical deficiencies with nimble footwork and legerdemain. Think of Gerald Davies or Barry John or Phil Bennett. All of them played at one time or another for Llanelli, Bennett for his entire career. Besides, if one region had an advantage in identity, it was the Scarlets, the clue being in their original 2003 name Llanelli Scarlets. To their credit, they ditched 'Llanelli' five years later in the interests of regionalism. But though when it started they had North Wales inserted into their responsibilities, they were never really anything but Llanelli – nickname, 'Scarlets' – by another name.

In too many years it has made next to no difference. Llanelli Scarlets were champions in 2003-04 and Scarlets never again until 2016-17. They had made the PRO12 play-offs only once before last season. In the first play-off season, 2009-10, they grimly finished ninth of ten. In between, the Ospreys won this league four times. They have been the best-placed Welsh region eight times to the Scarlets' four. The Blues have managed that distinction twice, the Dragons not at all. The burden is disproportionate.

Does this help explain why the Welsh regions tend to fail in Europe? Since the Cardiff club side made the inaugural Heineken Cup final in 1996, when English clubs were barred from participating by their own Rugby Football Union, no Welsh side has ever made the final. Since then the Irish have had six winners (Leinster three times, Munster twice, Ulster in 1999 during an English boycott) and three runners-up. On that basis, it is inaccurate and unfair for anyone in Wales to complain that the PRO12 does not do the job for them.

Anyway, perhaps there are signs of a change, even allowing for the Ospreys' repeated failure since 2010 to make even the quarter-finals. Given their 'domestic' success, Scarlets' European record was a largely unremarked feature of their season. At first glance third place in Pool Three is no great attainment. But the Scarlets easily beat Sale in Llanelli, itself an anti-plutocratic result. They went on to beat recent champions Toulon at home and drew there with the successful defending champions Saracens. In the away ties they gave Saracens and Toulon more bother than is usual and narrowly lost to Sale. All of which is just a way of indicating the Welsh European dearth need only be a protracted phase, not a permanent state of affairs.

It is certainly not the PRO12's problem, whatever its faults. The automatic qualification of one Italian no-hoper has henceforth ceased, meaning no one from Ireland, Wales or Scotland can any longer cry foul about being unjustly stuck in the second-tier Challenge Cup.

Idle fancy though it is, consider how the Scarlets might have gone in Europe if they by then had been playing the exhilarating rugby that gave them the irresistible momentum to run past, over and through both Leinster and Munster. The vehicle for that would be – is – the PRO12 and if it works for past European champions such as Leinster and Munster, there is no earthly reason it should not do so too for the Scarlets. A worthy Welsh European challenge, never mind a Welsh European champion, is way overdue.

BELOW Scarlets' Rhys Patchell (No. 10) and James Davies hold up Munster's Francis Saili during the PRO12 final in Dublin.

FACING PAGE Tadhg Beirne of Scarlets beats Alun Wyn Jones of Ospreys to the ball at Liberty Stadium. Ospreys are the most successful Welsh side PRO12-wise, having won four titles and been best-placed region on eight occasions.

The world is looking rather *surreal* at the moment. Which is why the PROFIT Hunters' skills are more important than ever.

THE ARTEMIS HUNTERS spurn the well-trodden path. Opting instead to explore the further reaches of Profit territory. Years of experience in doing so have taught them that they can rely on their agility of mind and fleetness of foot in the face of the unexpected. Invaluable attributes in an economic and geopolitical landscape as surreal as the one we find ourselves in today.

Please remember that past performance should not be seen as a guide to future performance. The value of an investment, and the income from it, can fall and rise because of stockmarket and currency movements and you may not get back the amount originally invested.

ARTEMIS
The PROFIT Hunter

Exeter on Top of the World
THE AVIVA PREMIERSHIP

by **CHRIS HEWETT**

Exeter did it by building from the bottom up rather than the top down, steering well clear of stellar names in favour of inspired talent-spotting and cutting-edge youth development

Comparisons can be every bit as odious in rugby union as in any other field of human endeavour: when changes of style and circumstance are taken into account, who can say for sure that Jeremy Guscott was a better outside centre than Danie Gerber, or that Richie McCaw had more going for him as an open-side flanker for all the ages than Michael Jones? Yet there is something so sweet-scented, so gloriously ambrosial, about the rise of Exeter from top-flight no-hopers to national champions in the space of seven

seasons that it is tempting to rank their achievement above those of any of their predecessors. Yes, that includes the Premiership-European double-winning exploits of Leicester, Wasps and, most recently, Saracens.

It is perfectly reasonable to place Sale's one-off triumph in 2005-06 in an elevated position: for one thing, few people thought them capable of breaking the Leicester-Wasps duopoly that had straddled the closing years of the 20th century and the early ones of the 21st; for another, they did English rugby a valuable service by proving it possible to finish top of the table AND stay ahead of the rest in the knockout phase. It is also right and proper to acknowledge the extraordinary success of Newcastle in winning the inaugural title in 1997-98, mere months after promotion from the second tier. But Philippe Saint-André and Rob Andrew, the respective directors of rugby in those northern outposts, spent an awful lot of money in piecing together squads capable of securing the prize. Exeter did it by building from the bottom up rather than the top down, steering well clear of stellar names in favour of inspired talent-spotting and cutting-edge youth development. When they went shopping for foreign internationals, they signed Dave Dennis and Michele Campagnaro, not Luke McAlister or Va'aiga Tuigamala.

As an outside half, McAlister was – and remains, down there in southern France – infinitely more celebrated than Gareth Steenson will ever be, but did the All Black from Waitara make more of an impact on rugby life in these islands than the uncapped Ulsterman from Dungannon? Please. McAlister was some player back in the mid-noughties. Too good for his own good, according to some. But Steenson was on the field, kicking goals from all points of the compass, when Exeter won promotion at the expense of Bristol in the late spring of 2010 and was still on the field (at Twickenham rather than the Memorial Ground) and still kicking goals in the late spring of 2017. The last of those goals, from a scrum penalty awarded against the Wasps loose-head prop Matt

LEFT Exeter celebrate as Sam Simmonds (hidden) scores the winning try against Saracens in the Sandy Park semi-final with seconds left on the clock after Henry Slade's huge touchfinding penalty had put Chiefs just metres from the Sarries line.

PAGE 95 Josh Bassett cannot stop Jack Nowell from going over for Exeter's first try of the Aviva Premiership final at Twickenham.

Mullan at the back end of a wonderfully competitive final that could not be decided without the aid of extra time, was the one that earned the Chiefs both a 23-20 victory and their hearts' desire, but there have been so many successful kicks over the seasons. Almost 500 of them, some of which have won games every bit as important to the club's wellbeing, if not quite as glamorous, as the showpiece event in southwest London.

Steenson is revered by Exeter supporters as one of the remaining 'originals': like the full back Phil Dollman and the prop Ben Moon, both of whom were alongside him in the starting line-up on final day, he was giving everything of himself when the Chiefs were travelling to Bedford, Moseley and Rotherham rather than Bath, Harlequins and Northampton. More than anyone, he has been the conscience of the team. As the head coach Rob Baxter said a couple of Christmases back, as his side were just beginning to look like serious title contenders: 'A culture doesn't just sit there, unchanging from season to season. It evolves. When I look at the club and the feeling within it now, it's very different to five years ago. Why? Because the senior players here understood the importance of growing up. They appreciated the need to raise their levels, personally and collectively, if they were to keep pace with their own expectations. Gareth has been very important in that. Some professional players look at Exeter and see it as a nice, friendly place to be. If I'm the only person telling people that it's more than that, it doesn't work. We need people like Gareth to drive standards, and he does.'

There was a notion at the start of the season that Steenson, having started every Premiership game of the preceding two campaigns, had done his bit, and that one of the bright young things, the much-talked-about Henry Slade, should be charged with the task of moving things forward from No. 10. If this was a firm policy statement, it lasted about as long as the Conservative Party's 'dementia tax' plan. Steenson was back in the thick of it before autumn was out and from the moment they put a rough start behind them by recording a bonus-point victory over Newcastle at Kingston Park in mid-November, the Chiefs had themselves a ball. Indeed, they did not lose another Premiership game, be it round-robin or knockout. They won 15 and drew two, against Saracens and Wasps – the other clubs in a three-team breakaway at the top of the English game.

It was possible to predict at the end of the 2015-16 campaign that threequarters of the league would spend 2016-17 in catch-up mode. So it proved. Saracens, who began the league programme as reigning

champions, knew they would be hit particularly hard by international demands, but their 'glue' players – the error-free wing Chris Wyles, the masterful kicking half back Richard Wigglesworth, the energetic back-five forward Michael Rhodes, the indefatigable flanker-cum-No. 8 Jackson Wray – combined with a range of newcomers, from the button-bright youngster Alex Lozowski to the rumbustious old Springbok wrecking ball Schalk Burger, in a classic make-do-and-mend operation. Strikingly, their vital statistics over the stretch of the 22 regular-season fixtures were much the same as they had been a year previously: they won 16 of their games, as opposed to 17, scored 66 tries rather than 60 and picked up 11 bonus points, a difference of one. That they finished third on the log rather than first was a reflection of the tightness of the race.

Wasps, boasting more rock stars than Glastonbury thanks to the arrivals of Willie le Roux from Springbok land, the bewilderingly brilliant Kurtley Beale from Wallaby country and a playmaker by the name of Danny Cipriani from the English

ABOVE Ellis Genge on the rampage for Leicester against Sale Sharks at Welford Road. The loose-head went on to start both Tests against Argentina on England's summer tour.

LEFT Chris Robshaw finds himself at the centre of things against Bristol at Twickenham on the season's opening Saturday. Bristol were 14-3 up, but Quins eventually won 21-19 to set the Premiership returners on a downward trajectory they could not reverse.

shires, were the most prolific team in attack – only
Exeter pushed them close – and, of those sides
aspiring to be better than also-rans, the most
generous in defence. If this said something for
their chosen style of broken-field rugby, a 'you
score two and we'll score three' mentality geared
towards maximum entertainment, it also exposed
the fault line running through their system.
Numbers rarely tell the whole story, but the leaking
of almost 23 points a game is not a good look for a
team with an eye on the prize.

Once it became clear that Bristol had failed to
recruit nearly strongly enough to survive their first
season back in the big time – despite a bright start
against Harlequins on the opening day, this
realisation dawned depressingly quickly – there was
something distinctly ho-hum about the remaining
two-thirds of the contenders. At least Leicester
were interesting in a macabre kind of way: the
transformation of Welford Road from fortress to
Wendy house cost both Richard Cockerill and
Aaron Mauger their positions at the top end of the
coaching roster and for much of the piece, it
looked as though the Midlanders would fall short

ABOVE Exeter fly half Gareth Steenson converts the extra-time
penalty that brought the Premiership title to Sandy Park.

RIGHT Steenson and Jack Yeandle raise the Premiership trophy as
Chiefs celebrate their 23-20 victory over Wasps at Twickenham.

of the top four for the first time in 13 years. But they are nothing if not determined. With Ellis Genge, the young front-row signing from Bristol, performing with an intensity bordering on the scary and the former Leeds lock Dom Barrow putting himself about with wild abandon, they rediscovered enough of the old Tigerish ferocity to make a late run into the semi-finals at the expense of a soft-centred Bath, whose assessment of their own capacity turned out to be just a little inflated.

Newcastle, their rugby transformed by David Walder's coaching of the attacking game and a super-fast playing surface on Tyneside, had their fair share of encouraging moments, as did Sale, who struggled to overcome the loss of Cipriani but emerged ahead of the game by throwing the teenaged Curry twins, Tom and Ben, into grown-up rugby and seeing them prosper in the most eye-catching of ways. Harlequins? Nothing much to report, apart from some valedictory virtuosity from the retiring outside half Nick Evans and the startling progress of the tight-head prop Kyle Sinckler, who has 'World Cup 2019' stamped all over his bull-necked body. Northampton and Gloucester? Not up to it, by a long chalk. Worcester? Much improved under the wise management of Gary Gold, but still eleventh out of 12.

There may be good reasons to believe that one of Leicester or Bath have it in them to break the three-handed stranglehold imposed on the Premiership by the leading trio, but they are not immediately apparent. There again, nothing is impossible. Ask Exeter, the first West Country club to call themselves English champions in the professional era. Who'd have thought it? Not Bruce Craig or Stephen Lansdown or any of the other businessmen who have pumped money into Bath, Bristol and Gloucester over the last 20-odd years, that's for sure.

Saracens Retain Control
THE EUROPEAN CHAMPIONS CUP

by DAVID HANDS

But in the final Saracens were always in the lead as they became the fourth club to record back-to-back European Cup wins, following Leicester (2001-02), Leinster (2011-12) and Toulon (2013-15)

Two names ran through the 2016-17 European Champions Cup, those of Saracens – the winners for the second year in succession – and Anthony Foley. Saracens have made themselves the leaders of the second generation of professional rugby in Europe, while the death of Foley, Munster's coach, at the age of 42 on the weekend of the first round of pool matches placed any and all sporting achievements in the sharpest of perspectives.

The former Munster and Ireland No. 8 died of a heart condition in a Paris hotel room on the eve of Munster's game against Racing 92, a genuine tragedy (rather than merely a sporting one) for Olive, his wife, his two sons, Tony and Dan, and for the families. Yet Olive and Tony had the fortitude to appear at the final seven months later to present the award for the player of the tournament, renamed the Anthony Foley Trophy, to Owen Farrell after Saracens had beaten Clermont Auvergne 28-17 at BT Murrayfield.

Moreover Foley's passing engendered such a response within his province that it swept Munster to the European semi-finals (where they were undone by Saracens) and the final of the Guinness PRO12. That the Irish province will build on that flood tide of emotion must be taken as read but the market leaders remain Saracens. Victory over Clermont was their eighteenth European game in succession without defeat over two seasons, a record, though they needed a last-minute conversion from Farrell for a 22-22 draw in Llanelli in the second pool meeting with the Scarlets.

Yet so much room remains for improvement in the Saracens squad. Such is the youthful talent they have at their disposal, together with the external experience gathered from their contribution to England and the British & Irish Lions, that it will take an exceptional team to overcome them. Under the shrewd management of Mark McCall, their director of rugby, they have also renewed their coaching

BELOW Referee Mathieu Raynal signals a penalty try in the 21st minute at Welford Road as Glasgow Warriors beat the Tigers 43-0.

FACING PAGE Sarries' Chris Ashton opens the scoring in the final, in the process breaking the try-scoring record for the competition.

staff, and their representation on England's senior tour of Argentina during the summer and in England's Under 20 squad suggests more playing talent in the pipeline.

However, Munster's renaissance helped ensure that the knockout phase was not the Anglo-French carve-up of the preceding season. Four countries were represented in the quarter-finals, among them Scotland for whom the appearance of Glasgow Warriors was a first and a fitting tribute to the coaching of Gregor Townsend before his departure to become Scotland's head coach. Not only that, Glasgow, on the opening night of the 2016-17 tournament, indicated that the old order was changing by despatching Leicester 42-13 at Scotstoun. When the Warriors ended the pool phase with a 43-0 win over Leicester at Welford Road, it confirmed a worst ever European season for the Tigers, who had dismissed their director of rugby, Richard Cockerill, earlier in the month.

Other results from the opening weekend included a record points haul for Wasps in their 82-14 despatch of Zebre and, more significantly, a 31-23 win for Saracens at Toulon, winners of the competition from 2013 to 2015. But the events of that weekend were completely overshadowed by Foley's death and the postponement of Munster's clash with Racing 92. A week later, discussion once again centred around Munster and their reaction 24 hours after Foley's funeral in Killaloe. It was nothing less than Foley would have wanted: a bonus-point 38-17 win over Glasgow, despite the loss in the first half of Keith Earls, the Ireland wing shown a red card for a dangerous tackle. Tyler Bleyendaal, the fly half from New Zealand with a South African name, led the way on his Champions Cup debut, his 16-point haul including the first try of the game.

Another New Zealander, Jimmy Gopperth, kicked the conversion that earned Wasps a 20-20 draw in Toulouse, but after two rounds the only side with a maximum ten points was Clermont. Almost inevitably, the French club faltered in round three although they claimed two losing bonus points in the 39-32 loss to Ulster in Belfast, scoring the last two tries through Nick Abendanon and Damien Chouly.

That would have given them some comfort; there was none for the two Midlands clubs, Northampton and Leicester. In their 100th European game, Northampton were sunk 37-10 on their own ground by Leinster, while Leicester were humiliated 38-0 by Munster at Thomond Park, their biggest ever margin of defeat in Europe. There was worse to come for Northampton in the reverse fixture a week later: they took a weakened side to Dublin and were duly thrashed 60-13. It was some consolation that, at the season's end, the Saints were able to fight their way past Stade Français in the play-offs and claim the twentieth and last place in the 2017-18 competition.

But the major controversy from the fourth round came in the west of Ireland. A week earlier, Wasps had been forced to work extremely hard for their 32-17 win over Connacht in Coventry. Now, in Galway, they clung to an 18-13 lead as the seconds ticked away. Connacht then kicked a penalty to touch for a close-range line out, from which Naulia Dawai scored and Jack Carty kicked the acutely angled conversion for a 20-18 win. Few in the crowd realised, however, that this denouement should not have been allowed by the referee, France's Mathieu Raynal, himself an injury replacement in the final quarter for Jérôme Garcès.

John Muldoon, Connacht's captain, argued that a law amendment allowed for the penalty and subsequent line out to be taken, even after 80 minutes had passed, but that amendment did not apply in the northern hemisphere until August 2017. Even though they agreed that the referee had erred, European Professional Club Rugby (the tournament organisers) allowed the result to stand on the basis that Connacht could have scored from a tapped penalty or scrum. Wasps, understandably disappointed, accepted the verdict even though their own players had suggested on the pitch that time had elapsed; moreover the defeat cost them a home draw in the knockout phase.

It was not, overall, a wonderful weekend for players or officials, since in 20 European matches, six red cards and 29 yellows were handed out, three of the latter at Welford Road where a late 52-metre penalty by Owen Williams gave Leicester an 18-16 win over Munster and restored some measure of self-respect.

The rearranged match between Racing 92 and Munster was fitted in early in the new year, the Irish province winning 32-7; and after the dust settled on the final two pool rounds, the quarter-final draw paired Clermont with Toulon, Leinster with Wasps, Saracens with Glasgow and Munster with Toulouse.

BELOW Chris Wyles (second from bottom) rolls over the line for Saracens' second try against Munster in the Dublin semi-final.

FACING PAGE With the last kick of the game, Jack Carty snatches a 20-18 win for Connacht over Wasps in Galway.

Wasps may have been the form team in the Aviva Premiership but this cut little ice in Dublin, where they could not match the ball-winning capabilities of Leinster, 32-17 winners. Even if South African Willie le Roux had scored the try that was chalked off when he lost the ball in an extravagant dive for the line, Wasps would probably still have lost, such was Leinster's intensity.

Clermont won the all-French affair 29-9, Saracens were similarly inconvenienced by Glasgow (38-13) and Munster scored four tries in beating Toulouse 41-16. This earned them a 'home' semi-final – if playing in Dublin's Aviva Stadium can ever be described as home for the

ABOVE Clermont fly half Camille Lopez (centre) watches as one of his two second-half dropped goals finds its mark as the French side see off Leinster 27-22 in the semi-finals.

RIGHT Alex Goode flies in for Saracens' third try of the final to put daylight between the defending champions and Clermont with seven minutes left on the clock.

Munstermen – but midway through the second half, the contest had been resolved in favour of Saracens. The English champions defended magnificently before scoring second-half tries through Mako Vunipola and Chris Wyles, the late try by Ireland's C J Stander meaning little as Munster went down 26-10.

Similarly Clermont played Leinster on French soil, in Lyon, but were tested to the full before claiming a 27-22 win. How easy it looked for the French club as Peceli Yato and David Strettle scored early tries in a 15-0 lead, how much more difficult as Leinster came back to 15-12 and thought they had taken the lead through a Dan Leavy score. But play was brought back because of obstruction and, even though a fine try by Garry Ringrose took Leinster within two points, Clermont closed the deal through the goal-kicking of Camille Lopez.

But in the final Saracens were always in the lead as they became the fourth club to record back-to-back European Cup wins, following Leicester (2001-02), Leinster (2011-12) and Toulon (2013-15). It was an outstanding game of rugby during which Chris Ashton, the Saracens wing, scored his thirty-seventh European Cup try and thereby eclipsed the record held by Vincent Clerc of Toulouse. But the cushion came from Farrell's goal-kicking: after Ashton's score, the fly half converted another try by George Kruis, then kicked two second-half penalties as Clermont rallied with a try by Abendanon which, with Morgan Parra's conversion, brought them within a point.

But there was to be no fairy-tale ending for Clermont, for whom Rémi Lamerat had scored a try in the first half, converted by Parra (who also kicked a penalty on the hour). Alex Goode, the Saracens full back, scored their third try with seven minutes remaining, Farrell converted and nailed down the coffin lid with his third penalty for a 28-17 win, coincidentally the 100th European win by Saracens. For the fifth time Benjamin Kayser, Clermont's hooker, suffered defeat in a European final – with Stade Français in 2005, Leicester (2009) and Clermont (2013, 2015 and 2017).

As luck would have it, these two clubs have been drawn together in pool play for the 2017-18 tournament which concludes with a final at a new venue, the San Mamés Stadium in Bilbao. This is the first time the organisers have gone outside the home unions, France and Italy, but given the enthusiastic reception for major club matches taken to Barcelona, the appetite in Spain is clearly there. Newcastle will play host to the 2019 finals, building on the good attendances at St James' Park during the 2015 World Cup and at a time when the playing fortunes of Newcastle Falcons seem more soundly based than at any time since 2000.

Gloucester Pay the Penalty
THE EUROPEAN CHALLENGE CUP

by HUGH GODWIN

A penalty by Burns made it 10-0, but it coincided with Gloucester's tight-head prop John Afoa limping off with a calf strain. A long evening of scrummaging hardship loomed ahead for the Cherry and Whites

The final of the Challenge Cup was held at Murrayfield in the seventh season of the two European competitions being brought to their conclusions in a single city across one weekend, and it offered a shot at redemption for two clubs who had endured troubled seasons. Gloucester finished in a dissatisfying ninth place in the Premiership, so the Cherry and Whites knew they needed to win this

ABOVE Centre Geoffrey Doumayrou cuts through the Gloucester defence to score. With Morné Steyn's conversion, Stade go 12 points clear with just nine minutes to go.

RIGHT Stade skipper Sergio Parisse gathers lock Hugh Pyle's (third from left) knock-down to run in for his side's first try of the Challenge Cup final at Murrayfield.

BELOW Jonny May intercepts and streaks away from the Stade cover to score for Gloucester after 13 minutes.

tournament if they were to claim the seventh and last English place in the 2017-18 Champions Cup. A hint of greater potential had been seen in Gloucester's Challenge Cup semi-final victory away to La Rochelle – inflicting the first home loss of the season on the table-toppers in France's Top 14 – but that came after Gloucester's head coach Laurie Fisher had resigned in early March, citing an 'unbelievable capitulation' in a Premiership match at home to Harlequins. Meanwhile, the offer of a substantial investment at Kingsholm from French-based businessman Mohed Altrad had been turned down by Gloucester's fellow Premiership clubs who decided there was a conflict of interest in Altrad's existing ownership of Montpellier.

Nevertheless, all of this seemed mild by comparison with the travails of Stade Français, who had qualified for the Champions Cup already

through their Top 14 position of seventh. A merger with Parisian neighbours Racing 92 had been announced to a shocked world by the clubs' owners in March, accompanied by brazen triumphalism, only to be swiftly abandoned in the face of fierce protests by fans and players. It made the mood of the Stade squad difficult to judge as they arrived in Edinburgh on a squally, rainy day in mid-May, not least because many of their star men were busy penning contracts elsewhere, and the head coach Gonzalo Quesada had lined up an end-of-season switch to Biarritz.

Still the French champions of a mere two years ago were packed with talent, from Jules Plisson and Will Genia as the half backs to evergreen captain Sergio Parisse at No. 8, as the club chased its first European title. Pascal Papé and Josaia Raisuqe, the lock and wing respectively, were suspended. For their part, Gloucester were hoping to be the second club after Harlequins to win the Challenge Cup for a third time, but they had Jacob Rowan and Matt Kvesic missing from the back row, which threw a brighter spotlight on Ross Moriarty, the Welsh flanker and Gloucester's only representative in the original squad for the British & Irish Lions tour, although scrum half Greig Laidlaw had just become the second as a call-up to replace Ben Youngs. This would be Laidlaw's farewell appearance for Gloucester, after three seasons at Kingsholm and eight with Edinburgh, before his move to Clermont Auvergne. But a recent injury meant the nuggety Borderer was confined to the bench behind Willi Heinz, the 30-year-old New Zealander and stand-in captain – and this would be a pivotal selection in an eventful match.

Gloucester enjoyed a first half-hour of no little encouragement, as they built a 10-3 lead, and yet there were ominous signs along the way. With 13 minutes gone, Parisse's lavish behind-the-back pass to Plisson earned gasps of admiration but, one pass later, the inside centre Jonathan Danty's delivery to Jono Ross – the flanker joining Sale Sharks in the summer – was anticipated for an interception by Jonny May, and the England wing sprinted 75 metres for a clever try converted by fly half Billy Burns.

A penalty by Burns made it 10-0, but it coincided with Gloucester's tight-head prop John Afoa limping off with a calf strain. A long evening of scrummaging hardship loomed ahead for the Cherry and Whites, not helped by the questionable but legal ruse by Stade of withdrawing their French international No. 3 Rabah Slimani for tactical reasons at half-time, only to restore him (and not the more obvious, unused

substitute Zurabi Zhvania) on the left side of the scrum during the second half when the starting No. 1, Heinke van der Merwe, sustained a bloody nick to the forehead. Eyebrows rose in the Murrayfield press box and television commentators' booth, partly due to the recent memory of Slimani's involvement in the controversial France-Wales match earlier in the season, but Gloucester raised no complaint.

The first half ended with the teams level at 10-all, and Gloucester a man down. Plisson kicked a 50-metre penalty into the wind, then, playing with an advantage, the clever Genia spotted Heinz out of position. He chipped a ball towards the Gloucester posts where big Stade lock Hugh Pyle outreached Burns and the rapidly recovering Heinz to bat the ball down for Parisse to score a try converted by Plisson. Maybe this led to frustration boiling in Heinz when, in Gloucester's next attack, he was penalised and sent to the sin-bin for a shove in the face of Plisson in the follow-through of an attempted charge-down. Or it may have been a simple misjudgment. 'You have to be squeaky-clean these days, the way the game is being refereed' was Heinz's sorrowful verdict afterwards.

There was a brawl near the touch line involving half the players, in response to a ruck clear-out, but no scoring during Heinz's absence and when his ten minutes were up, Laidlaw made his entry. Plisson missed a penalty for Stade, but Gloucester regretted the latest of three knock-ons in fine attacking positions – blaming the wet ball, no doubt. Next came a calamitous period for Gloucester. First, the Stade Français full back Hugo Bonneval got away with a block on his opposite number Tom Marshall as the Gloucester man chased a Laidlaw box kick and grounded it a fraction too late, as it crossed the dead-ball line. Then, with 57 minutes played, Danty ran in Stade's second try. A pass by Marshall was intercepted by Djibril Camara, and Bonneval, with a sumptuous offload out of a tackle, gave the scoring pass to the barrelling Danty.

The penalty count against Gloucester was mounting, at the scrum and elsewhere, even if the gap in points was a manageable five with just over ten minutes remaining. Morné Steyn, the ex-Springbok on for Plisson, missed a penalty, but the knockout blow was landed in the 71st minute. Stade had a line out 25 metres from Gloucester's goal line, and attacked right to left. Billy Twelvetrees, on for Laidlaw's fellow Scottish international Matt Scott, flew up hard in defence but in doing so left a problematic dog-leg inside him. Once Geoffrey Doumayrou, the Stade centre, had sidestepped past Mark Atkinson, he had only a couple of tired forwards to beat on an exultant run-in. Steyn added the conversion and a further penalty, from yet another struggling Gloucester scrum, and although Moriarty finished a move of nine phases with a try from the replacement hooker Darren Dawidiuk's line break on Laidlaw's shoulder, it was too late to affect the result.

Post-match, in a marquee in the Murrayfield car park, an ebullient Quesada took press questions alongside a more circumspect Parisse. 'I do everything with my heart,' said Quesada, the former Argentina fly half, 'and when you live too much through your work, it can be a problem. So I'm not going to cry in front of you guys, but it's a special evening. Just imagine what it has been like for the players, not knowing if the club was going to survive. Now, to beat an English team in Scotland, and to finish the season fitter than an English team, shows our quality. I was just a privileged witness of what was going on.'

Parisse, who was looking forward to a summer of being rested from playing for Italy, said: 'When the merger did not happen, and the club started looking for a buyer, the best thing for the players was to be good on the pitch. These players have written a page of the Stade Français story. We've done our best and we'll see what happens now. For the time being it's just a joy – the first European title for the club.'

Quesada's Gloucester counterpart, director of rugby David Humphreys, made no complaint over the Slimani scenario, and said: 'Congratulations to Stade on their win. Our character cannot be questioned, but it's very hard to play any rugby when you have no ball. The scrum struggled and we gave away too many penalties and we just didn't play well enough.'

FACING PAGE Tom Marshall, Gloucester's full back, just fails to touch the ball down for a try before it reaches the dead-ball line. A moment or two later, Jonathan Danty scored for Stade at the other end.

BELOW Jubilant Stade captain Sergio Parisse leads the winners' celebrations.

4

REVIEW OF THE
SEASON 2016-17

To the Brink of History
THE RBS 6 NATIONS CHAMPIONSHIP

by CHRIS JONES

A Jonathan Joseph hat-trick against Scotland gave England the title. Jones's side scored seven tries in a 61-21 triumph to equal New Zealand's record for a major rugby nation of 18 victories in a row

England retained the title but came up short in their bid for back-to-back Grand Slams in a 2017 RBS 6 Nations Championship played out against the backdrop of the impending British & Irish Lions tour to New Zealand. While the make-up of the Lions squad was a major topic of discussion throughout the competition along with the introduction of bonus points, the influence of national coaches also warranted plenty of column inches, with Eddie Jones, the England head coach, grabbing the majority of the attention, particularly when new Italian coach Conor O'Shea brought his men to Twickenham.

England won the game, but Italy were the tactical winners, with Jones responding to the Azzurri refusal to create a ruck by claiming it amounted to anti-rugby. The neutrals were fascinated by Italy's tactic of not committing anyone to the breakdown, which meant an absence of an offside line and Italy players were to be found amongst the bemused England backs causing all kinds of confusion. England flanker James Haskell attracted negative comments after asking the referee what his team could and couldn't do when faced with this puzzle. Haskell should have been quicker on the uptake as Wasps had used the same tactic during a recent European Champions Cup game.

In the end Italy finished the match well beaten and O'Shea's first season failed to provide a win, meaning they had to pick up the dreaded Wooden Spoon yet again. Besides Jones and O'Shea, there

RIGHT Jonathan Joseph slices through the Scotland back line to score the first of his three tries as England win at Twickenham to retain their title and equal New Zealand's run of 18 Test wins.

was also interest in Scotland's Vern Cotter and Rob Howley of Wales. Cotter was in his final season as Scotland coach following the news that Gregor Townsend would be taking over at the end of the campaign, while Howley was once against cast in the role of stand-in Wales coach as Warren Gatland assumed the head coach duties with the Lions. Howley's tenure included having to watch his men lose to France in Paris in the first 100-minute match!

The Scottish players were determined to mark Cotter's last season with real success, and it all started so well with Stuart Hogg's two first-half tries fashioning a 27-22 win at BT Murrayfield over Ireland. The Scots don't normally win their opening Six Nations match, but with Hogg's double and a try from Alex Dunbar they led 21-8 at half-time, with Keith Earls having crossed for the visitors. Ireland did close the gap but never managed to get ahead of the highly motivated Scots.

England opened their defence of the title with former rugby league star Ben Te'o going over for a vital try in a 19-16 win over France at Twickenham. This result took England's run of wins to 15 as they chased New Zealand's world record of 18 on the trot which was ended by Ireland in Chicago in November 2016. Rabah Slimani got the game's opening try after the teams had relied on the boot to keep the scoreboard

moving. Jones has never been afraid to make changes, and having taken off captain Dylan Hartley, he brought on Te'o for George Ford.

Leigh Halfpenny was the key man as Wales scored 30 unanswered second-half points in a 33-7 victory over Italy at the Stadio Olimpico. Scrum half Edoardo Gori's converted try put Italy 7-0 up and the locals were dreaming of a new era under O'Shea, but Halfpenny's boot kept hurting them. Then Jonathan Davies, Liam Williams and George North delivered the tries that made it a very successful second half for Howley's men.

Things really went downhill quickly for O'Shea and his Italian players as they then suffered a 63-10 home defeat by Ireland. CJ Stander and Craig Gilroy both crossed for hat-tricks as Ireland registered the first winning bonus point in Six Nations history. That bonus point for four tries was collected before half-time! Donnacha Ryan collected a yellow card and Italy benefited from a penalty try on an otherwise forgettable occasion for the Azzurri. Garry Ringrose also scored a try for the Irish and showed that he was a real talent.

England were in real trouble against Wales in Cardiff, and when the ball was kicked downfield late in the game by Jonathan Davies it offered the reigning champions one last chance to save themselves. They took it, with a fantastic pass from Owen Farrell enabling Elliot Daly to get on the outside of his opposite number to squeeze in at the corner and secure a 21-16 win. Liam Williams' try and 11 points from Halfpenny had put Wales 16-11 up with less than ten minutes left. Ben Youngs had scored an early England try and Farrell kept them in touch before initiating that late score; then he fired over the conversion for good measure.

Stuart Hogg was continuing his brilliant form from the 2016 championship and scored a further try for Scotland in Paris. However, a 17-point haul from Camille Lopez provided the bulk of the French scoring in a 22-16 win. Gaël Fickou's try had given France a 13-11 half-time lead and Lopez was on target to deny the Scots, who were showing consistent form in the championship at home and away. This was confirmed in the next round as Tim Visser scored a second-half try to ensure they would end up comfortable 29-13 winners over Wales at BT Murrayfield. Finn Russell's boot and a try from Tommy Seymour kept that smile on Cotter's face as he headed to Twickenham chasing a first Triple Crown since 1990.

Ireland showed they had no intention of becoming also-rans, by defeating France 19-9 in Dublin despite going down 6-0 early in the match. Conor Murray, confirming his position as the leading candidate for the Lions No. 9 jersey, got a try and Johnny Sexton, fit to return to the No. 10 role, kicked 11 points.

That match was 'normal' compared to what happened at Twickenham where England came up against those 'no ruck' tactics employed by Italy. England were 10-5 down but scored five second-half tries to enable Jones to come into the press conference and rip Italy apart for the way they played.

George North, whose problems with concussion had been such a concern earlier in the season, scored a try in each half as Wales eased the pressure on Howley by defeating Ireland 22-9 in Cardiff. It was a result

that meant England would claim a second successive title with victory over Scotland at Twickenham. By avoiding defeat, Wales ended the threat of a third successive loss – something they had not suffered for a decade. Jamie Roberts crashed over three minutes from time and Welsh fans could celebrate a much needed win.

France beat Italy 40-18 in Rome. Sergio Parisse's early try suggested an upset might be on the cards. However, Les Bleus bounced back with four tries, including a long-range effort finished by Fickou. Virimi Vakatawa, Louis Picamoles and Brice Dulin ensured a bonus point, while Angelo Esposito got a try for Italy.

A Jonathan Joseph hat-trick against a shell-shocked Scotland gave England the title and kept their hopes of another Grand

ABOVE Wayne Barnes signals a try to France (scored by Damien Chouly, hidden) against Wales, some 20 minutes into overtime in Paris.

RIGHT Iain Henderson scores the only try of the match as Ireland win in Dublin to deny England a Grand Slam and the outright win record.

Slam bid alive. Jones's side scored seven tries in a 61-21 triumph to equal New Zealand's record for a major rugby nation of 18 victories in a row. Fraser Brown collected a yellow card, while Stuart Hogg and his replacement Mark Bennett were injured as England set a new record of 11 wins in a row in the Six Nations. Anthony Watson, fit-again Billy Vunipola and Danny Care with two piled on the England tries, while Huw Jones scored two of Scotland's three tries on a day when they came a distant second.

Scotland ensured Cotter at least finished with a win as they ended the campaign with a 29-0 victory over Italy, with Finn Russell, Matt Scott, Tim Visser and Tommy Seymour scoring tries as the home side finished with three wins. The Scots ended up fourth in the table despite having the same number of points as Ireland and France who were second and third respectively. The bad news for O'Shea was that the setback meant Italy had lost 12 in a row in the championship.

The next two games on Super Saturday grabbed the headlines for different reasons. Damien Chouly's try in the 100th minute converted by Camille Lopez gave France a 20-18 victory over Wales in Paris. Referee Wayne Barnes played his part in an amazing match that featured 20 minutes of added time during which the French camped on the Welsh line, receiving numerous penalties which saw them opt for scrums as they chased the try to win the match. Halfpenny's six penalties had put Wales 18-13 up when normal time ended. A Rémi Lamerat try had helped put France ahead but Halfpenny's boot kept bringing the Welsh back into a contest that left everyone breathless and shaking their heads.

And so it came down to the final match in Dublin to decide the Slam, and England, as had happened all too often, failed to handle the pressure of being favourites in Dublin. Iain Henderson scored the only try of the game in a 13-9 Ireland victory over the champions which secured the home side second place and ensured a strong presence on the Lions tour. The loss meant England lifted the trophy in a rather subdued ceremony. Ireland won despite missing the injured Murray and Jamie Heaslip and were indebted to a man-of-the-match performance from Peter O'Mahony. England's defeat meant they remained joint record holders with New Zealand with 18 wins in a row – with the Irish responsible for both runs coming to an end!

The Club Scene
ENGLAND: IRISH BOUNCE BACK

by **NEALE HARVEY**

Irish began their campaign with a hard-fought victory over the previous season's play-off finalists Doncaster and never looked back. Seventeen straight wins followed

Coming off the back of a 2015-16 campaign in which they had conspired to get pretty much every major decision wrong and were duly relegated from the Aviva Premiership, London Irish atoned in splendid style under director of rugby Nick Kennedy to win the Greene King IPA Championship at the first attempt and secure an early return to club rugby's top table. Former lock and club favourite Kennedy had succeeded hapless New Zealander Tom Coventry, who was jettisoned at the end of an abysmal lone year at the helm, having failed to understand the demands of the Premiership or the tactics required to ensure survival. All-singing, all-dancing rugby may suit All Blacks weaned on a diet of dash, but the Exiles possessed neither the personnel nor the nous to make that sort of adjustment and paid the ultimate price.

In their hour of need following demotion, Irish wisely opted to turn back the clock. Another former player, 1995 South African World Cup-winning centre Brendan Venter, was whistled back north to assist as technical director alongside Kennedy, while three more ex-playing heroes in Paul Hodgson, Declan Danaher and George Skivington were promoted from the academy. All were well suited, with the club firmly in their hearts, and the move paid off handsomely.

Irish began their campaign with a hard-fought victory over the previous season's play-off finalists Doncaster and never looked back. Seventeen straight wins followed before fast-rising Jersey inflicted a shock 15-11 league defeat on the Exiles in late March – the solitary blemish on an otherwise perfect card as Irish roared into the play-offs 17 points clear before defeating Doncaster in the semis and Yorkshire Carnegie both home and away in the final to leave emotional boss Kennedy ecstatic. The former England man said: 'The Premiership is where this club belongs. My overriding emotions are relief and happiness but we know we have a lot of work to do because we're a year off the pace. We haven't been in the Premiership for a season and we were the worst team in the league then. Now everything has shifted on a year and we must up our standards. But we aim to hit all our targets and we're hungry to prove ourselves worthy in the Premiership.'

Kennedy is right to be cautious. As Bristol proved last season, having a wad of cash does not guarantee anything – and Irish are certainly no Bristol when it comes to finances. In fact, their annual turnover was one of the lowest the last time they were in the Premiership and, despite making a number of decent signings, they require urgent new investment.

Mick Crossan, Irish's president and major benefactor, warned: 'The challenge is to stay in the Premiership and build on the spirit we've created in the Championship. In that respect, taking a step back has not been the worst thing. But financially relegation has been tough and if we want to build London Irish back to where it was, we need more people investing.

'Personally, I need people to help me with the bills. My bank balance looked a lot better before I took over London Irish three years ago and my wife will fully testify to that, but I took on a challenge and I've always done that. Sometimes your heart rules your head and London Irish is a passion I'll never waver from, but we now need more help funding-wise.

'We've got a fantastic training facility at Hazelwood, one that's hosted NFL teams, England Rugby, the All Blacks and many other national teams, and we're in the throes of doing a deal with Brentford FC for a return to London, so things are looking much rosier. But it's vital we find new backers because I can't keep funding losses of £3 million and we need to share the pain.'

As Irish set out on their long journey to recapture the glory days that saw them reach the 2009 Premiership final and make an impact in Europe, there was no end to the suffering elsewhere in the Championship where a long battle to keep historic London Welsh afloat ended in abject failure. Sadly, their demise came as no real surprise to those who report regularly on Championship matters, as a mixture of wildly overinflated ambition that had already resulted in two failed spells in the Premiership meant more good money followed bad, with inevitable results. Three winding-up petitions were staved off before London Welsh finally admitted defeat in December by going into voluntary liquidation. And any hope of continuing in Level 2 as a new club was extinguished by the RFU in the new year as the Exiles failed to satisfy all the guarantees. As a result, players were laid off and their results expunged, leaving careworn supporters to hope for a rebirth in Level 9 after belatedly joining forces with the London Welsh Amateurs.

Whilst London Welsh can offer textbook authority on how to mismanage finances, the other side of the coin produced a magnificent success story as promoted Richmond showed what could be done on a modest budget by remaining part-time and staying up. Nor did they rely on London Welsh's demise to survive, winning five of their games to finish above Rotherham.

Doncaster enjoyed another consistent season under wily Welshman Clive Griffiths, reaching the play-offs for the second year running before losing to London Irish. And a major shout-out must go to Ealing Trailfinders, who achieved their highest ever placing in third. Alex Codling, Ealing's head coach, said: 'It was a really positive year and we were delighted to reach the semi-finals of the British & Irish Cup as well, so we'll reset now and look to push on again.'

Jersey enjoyed a fine season in which they were not just content to beat London Irish once and finish fifth but defeated the Exiles for a second time to reach the final of the British & Irish Cup. Sadly, their hopes of lifting silverware were dashed by a strong Munster A side but, under the astute management of Harvey Biljon, the Reds are surely destined to come again.

With no relegation due to the expulsion of London Welsh, Hartpury College will fill the Championship gap next season after a stellar National One campaign that saw them go through the season unbeaten. Only runners-up Plymouth managed to push the

PAGES 122-123 London Irish celebrate after winning the second leg of the Greene King IPA Championship final against Yorkshire Carnegie – and promotion – at the Madejski Stadium.

BELOW Ciaran Hearn crosses for Irish in the first minute of the second leg against Yorkshire Carnegie. The Exiles won the match 55-48.

FACING PAGE Action from the London Welsh v London Scottish clash at Old Deer Park on Christmas Eve 2016, Welsh's last home game before their expulsion from the Championship.

Gloucestershire outfit close and they will begin the new National One season as one of the favourites, along with big-spending Coventry who are determined to put a disappointing campaign behind them. Meanwhile, Blaydon and Macclesfield were relegated, the latter after just one season in Level 3.

In the next tier down, one of the most exciting denouements in club rugby came in National Two South, where upwardly mobile Bishop's Stortford secured promotion with a game to spare, leaving Old Elthamians and Chinnor to slug it out for the play-off spot right to the bitter end, before the former prevailed on points difference to clinch a trip north to play Sale. An old boys' team they may be in name, but Old Elthamians possess land and money and have bold ambitions of becoming the fully professional 'Team for Kent'. They duly secured promotion in a thrilling 19-14 victory at Sale, leaving rugby director Gavin Lach to reflect: 'What we've achieved is unbelievable and everything's coming together. We've got 60 acres of land at Eltham College, the Championship is on our radar and now we're one step nearer.

'We're developing our ground and there's a huge opportunity within the county of Kent because the two nearest professional sides right now are Saracens and Harlequins. If Kent had a professional side playing good, attractive rugby I think the fan base would be unbelievable. No one's done it before so if we can make a decent fist of National One, why shouldn't it be us?'

Joining Stortford and Elthamians in National One next season will be Wirral-based Caldy, who whistled through National Two North, losing just two games along the way. There was little joy at the bottom of National Two, though, with Harrogate, Scunthorpe and Preston Grasshoppers demoted from the northern division, along with Barnes and Exmouth from the south. Promoted in their places were four National Three regional champions in Tonbridge Juddians, Old Redcliffians, Broadstreet and Huddersfield, along with play-off winners Wimbledon and Sheffield.

In the County Championship, there was to be no repeat of last year's triumph for Cornwall, who were downed 19-8 by fierce rivals Lancashire in the Bill Beaumont Division One Cup, while Leicestershire overcame Hampshire 39-7 to claim the Division Two title and Oxfordshire outscored Sussex by five tries to four to lift the Division Three crown after a 29-29 draw.

RFU Intermediate Cup honours went to West Leeds, who defeated Charlton Park 35-26, while Jonny Wilkinson's old side Farnham bagged the RFU Senior Vase with a convincing 37-15 win over Droitwich, and Goole edged a 31-24 cracker against Spartans to lift the RFU Junior Vase.

SCOTLAND: SWINGS AND ROUNDABOUTS

by ALAN LORIMER

With many of their BT Academy players training with Glasgow, Ayr, Scottish Rugby's club of the year, now operate at a level closer to the professional game

If the Guinness PRO12 table can be regarded as a health check on professional club rugby in Scotland, then the 2016-17 standings showing sixth and ninth end-of-season positions for Glasgow Warriors and Edinburgh respectively make for uncomfortable reading. The league results, however, are not the complete picture. The flip sides of mediocre PRO12 performances by the two Scottish clubs were Glasgow's first ever qualification for the knockout stage of the European Cup and Edinburgh's achievement in reaching the quarter-finals of the Challenge competition.

So imbued have Scottish rugby followers become to Edinburgh's mediocrity in the league over the past few seasons, that it was Glasgow's fall from the PRO12 top four that provided the real sense of disappointment. After five seasons of reaching the play-offs, including lifting the title in 2015, Glasgow's hopes of continued Guinness glory faded towards the end of the 2016-17 championship when it soon became apparent that a late charge would not be enough to make up for poor mid-term results.

Put bluntly, Glasgow were victims of their own success. Glasgow supplied on average 13 players to the Scotland match-day squads, and without the strength in depth Warriors struggled during the international windows. Moreover that lack of quality cover was all too apparent during injury-enforced absences to the likes of Finn Russell, Peter Horne, Alex Dunbar, Jonny Gray and Josh Strauss. Critics would argue that Glasgow should have foreseen this problem and signed up foreign players to ensure strong squads during international periods. Two problems stand in the way, however. One is limited funds to attract quality foreigners and the other is the need to ensure a high percentage of Scotland-qualified players, for the simple reason that there are only two professional teams to supply the bulk of the national side.

Glasgow's PRO12 season reflected this lack of depth, the dips in form showing up during Scotland's international campaigns and the peaks occurring when the squad was back to full strength. It is of course a pattern experienced by most teams, but for Glasgow it was the sheer number of players called up for international duty that exacerbated the problem and ultimately scuppered the Scotstoun club's league chances. Still, the necessity to field younger and less experienced players accelerated the development of Matt Fagerson, the teenage younger brother of Zander Fagerson, fellow back-row Matt Smith and centre Nick Grigg, the last-mentioned becoming one of Glasgow's top performers. The other player to make a big impact was winger Lee Jones, who won four Scotland caps in 2012 before being shunned.

With most of their international players available for the European Champions Cup, Glasgow competed strongly, Warriors making a statement of intent in their opening match against Leicester Tigers at Scotstoun in recording a 42-13 win. A brace of losses to Munster was balanced by back-to-back victories over Racing 92 and then in the final pool match Warriors again broke loose against a demoralised Tigers team at Welford Road, winning 43-0 to secure a quarter-final place against Saracens.

> **FACING PAGE** Glasgow Warriors No. 8 Matt Fagerson is wrapped up against Edinburgh at Scotstoun in the last regular round of 2016-17 Guinness PRO12 games.
>
> **BELOW** Gregor Townsend has now left Glasgow to take up the post of head coach of the Scotland national team.

Glasgow's date with the defending champions at Allianz Park, however, proved to be a step too far. Warriors lost their co-captain, Jonny Gray, early in the match, after a collision with Owen Farrell's elbow, and without a similar-calibre replacement Glasgow struggled in the forward battle, while behind the scrum they could not make headway against a strangulating Saracens defence.

Even so Glasgow were only 14-8 down early in the second half, but once Saracens began to unload their strong bench in the final quarter Warriors collapsed, once again exposed by a critical lack of depth among the replacements. Henry Pyrgos, the Glasgow co-captain, hinted as much after the match, when he said: 'We were in the game for 60 minutes but they were ruthless in the last 20.' Pyrgos, however, recognised that this was a new and important step his side had taken. 'This is the start for us as a club, the first time in the knockouts and we want to be here again next year,' he stated.

Having exited from European competition, Glasgow entertained a slim hope of reaching the Guinness PRO12 play-offs. But six days after the defeat to Saracens, Warriors lost 10-7 to Munster in a last throw of the dice. Thereafter it was just a case of playing out their remaining matches, the last of which was against Edinburgh. This was a home game for Warriors and a farewell to Gregor Townsend as Glasgow coach. In the event Edinburgh spoiled the party by defeating their west coast rivals, but it mattered little as a packed Scotstoun rose as one to salute Townsend, who had brought a crowd-pleasing style to the club and taken his side to Guinness PRO12 supremacy along the way.

Edinburgh's winning performance against Glasgow was small comfort for a season that had gone badly for the east coast men. It had started wretchedly, and three weeks into the PRO12 season Edinburgh's South African-born coach, Alan Solomons, paid the price by being shown the door. Solomons had failed to lift Edinburgh from the nether regions of the PRO12 league during his tenure and his unimaginative style of play, allegedly the reason for Tim Visser's desire to move south, had never excited the home crowd. Assistant coach Duncan Hodge took over on an interim basis but his attempts to refloat a sunken ship were for the most part in vain. Then in the spring Scottish Rugby announced that Richard Cockerill, sacked earlier in the season by Leicester, was to take over as head coach, a recognition that Edinburgh needed a strongman at the helm to whip a permanently underperforming side into shape for the 2017-18 season.

If Edinburgh's PRO12 campaign can be viewed as something of a disaster, then their performances in Europe offered up hope that the capital outfit was far from a write-off. In the pool stage of the Challenge Cup Edinburgh won five out of their six matches, with home and away wins over Harlequins and Timisoara Saracens and a home victory over the eventual champions Stade Français, to secure a home quarter-final tie against La Rochelle. That was to be the limit of Edinburgh's progression. The Scottish capital side lost 32-22 to the then French Top 14 leaders, but overall the Challenge Cup campaign showed that Edinburgh have the capability to play winning rugby.

It may have been an uninspiring season for Edinburgh but individually a number of players helped lift the gloom, most notably back-rows Hamish Watson and Magnus Bradbury, hooker George Turner and second-row Ben Toolis among the forwards and Damien Hoyland and (in the latter part of the season) Sam Hidalgo-Clyne in the back line. Edinburgh undoubtedly suffered by having to do without their international props WP Nel and Alasdair Dickinson for almost the entire season, but the silver lining of this particular cloud was that understudies Allan Dell and Simon Berghan stepped up to fill the gap, the pair ultimately proving good enough to win Scotland caps.

With only two professional teams in Scotland, the next tier, the BT Premiership, is increasingly seen as the interface between the professional and amateur games. Rather late in the day Scotland has established four regional academies to cultivate potential professionals, and these are the players now beginning to populate the BT Premiership.

BT champions Ayr, who won the play-offs after finishing second in the league, illustrate what is happening at the sub-professional level. With many of their BT Academy players training with Glasgow, Ayr, Scottish Rugby's club of the year, now operate at a level closer to the professional game. A similar approach has been taken by play-off runners-up and league winners Melrose, third-placed Glasgow Hawks and the fourth member of this top quartet, Currie, all of whom provide a Scotland's Got Talent platform for would-be professional players.

While Melrose flew the flag for Borders rugby, Hawick and Gala, both small players among the bigger spenders these days, struggled in the championship. In the event Gala, the former club of the Scotland coach, Gregor Townsend, and Scotland's record cap holder, Chris Paterson, were relegated and replaced by Premiership first-timers Marr. Hawick, the alma mater of Scotland full back Stuart Hogg, only just survived in the top tier after winning a play-off against National League One runners-up Edinburgh Accies.

Ayr may have prevailed in the Premiership play-offs but in the BT Cup Melrose turned the tables on the Millbrae club by winning a closely contested match at BT Murrayfield, to send out a reminder that while the game in Scotland is becoming more concentrated in the central belt, Borders rugby, despite problems at Gala, still has a healthy heartbeat.

WALES: THE WEST IS BACK

by DAVID STEWART

That run took the Scarlets from eleventh to third in the league, finishing on 77 points behind only the two Irish provinces whom they would go on to vanquish in the play-offs

At last. The west is back. With no silverware in their cabinet since the Celtic League of 2003-04, the Scarlets defied many predictions by triumphing in the Guinness PRO12 play-offs, with a brand of rugby that had old-timers thinking wistfully back to the golden days of Carwyn James and Phil Bennett. Visits to Dublin on consecutive weekends at the end of May saw them gloriously defeat Leinster 27-15 in the semi-final (with 14 men for the entire second half, the unlucky Steffan Evans having been red-carded following a tackle) and then Munster 46-22 in the final. That a crowd of 44,000 were in attendance for the final suggests a league competition in better fettle than some detractors would assert.

And yet, it had all started so unpromisingly. Defeat in their first three games at home to Munster (their sole PRO12 defeat at Parc y Scarlets), then away to Edinburgh and Ulster saw harsh questions being asked in official circles of head coach Wayne Pivac. During his three years in the Llanelli area the Aucklander has displayed an impressive manner and a belief in the type of game plan which would bring success. It was some turnaround to win 17 of the next 19 league matches, dropping only the Ospreys derby during the Christmas period (19-9) and the away fixture to a Leinster squad with enviable depth during the Six Nations window.

That run took the Scarlets from eleventh to third in the league, finishing on 77 points behind only the two Irish provinces whom they would go on to vanquish in the play-offs. At full strength, their back line was one to savour: Johnny McNicholl, Liam Williams, Jonathan Davies, Scott Williams, Steff Evans, Rhys Patchell, Gareth Davies – a former Canterbury Crusader, and the rest (Evans being capped on the summer tour) all Welsh internationals. Much of the credit for the precise and thrilling flair they produced goes to former Lions fly half Stephen Jones. Jon Davies, player of the series on the 2017 Lions tour of New Zealand, said, 'He demands high standards. There are lots of backs here with international experience

RIGHT Left wing Steffan Evans scores Scarlets' second try in the 20th minute of the PRO12 final against Munster at the Aviva Stadium. The Scarlets ran out 46-22 winners.

and he insists that our levels don't slip in training. That has helped us become more accurate and take chances when they come along. Our conversion rate when we get behind teams has been pretty good.'

Other notable performers were the back row of outstanding Scottish skipper John Barclay, regularly featuring at No. 8, flanked by Aaron Shingler and Olympic Sevens player James 'Cub' Davies, younger brother of Jon (the 'Fox') – nicknames arising from the pub their parents ran. One to watch is young hooker Ryan Elias, who deputised for Ken Owens when the club captain missed the play-offs through injury, and went on to be another new cap on the Welsh tour. Titles aren't won without the tight five doing their stuff, and it was remarkable that Lewis Rawlins and Tadhg Beirne made so light of the absence of Jake Ball in the 'engine room' come the season's denouement. Scarlets' strong home form extended to the European Champions Cup, in which they beat Sale 28-11 and the mighty Toulon 22-21, and drew 22-22 with eventual winners Saracens. As top seeds in next's season's Pool Five, they again will face Toulon along with Bath and Benetton Treviso.

Ospreys were the last Welsh region to win the Celtic League, being champions in 2011-12. They also made the play-offs last term, finishing fourth in the PRO12 table, on 69 points. A comfortable opening saw them dispose of Zebre, Connacht and Benetton by big margins, before coming up short away to Leinster (31-19) and Ulster (9-7). Progress thereafter was bright, including the home and away double over Glasgow and Edinburgh, so that by the end of the Six Nations, they stood at won 13, lost four. A weak display at Benetton seemed to put the skids under their league campaign, with only a home win over Ulster to show from their last five games, the most painful loss being 40-17 to the neighbouring Scarlets in Llanelli. This poor form followed them into the play-offs where they succumbed to Munster 23-3 at Thomond Park.

Their European Challenge Cup campaign was brighter. A full set of wins over Grenoble, Lyon and Newcastle saw them top their pool, and they ran eventual winners Stade Français close (25-21) in the

Millennium Stadium quarter-final. Next term sees them back in the top tier of Europe, but a pool containing Saracens, plus last season's finalists Clermont as well as Northampton will be quite daunting. While the Swansea-based region were thrilled to have Alun Wyn Jones, Justin Tipuric, Rhys Webb and Dan Biggar all on the Lions tour, they will be sorry to lose newly capped English open-side Sam Underhill to Bath. New personnel include Cory Allen, Rob McCusker, and returning favourite James Hook, who will add depth to the midfield options next season alongside Biggar and Sam Davies, first capped in the Autumn Internationals. Against Samoa in June Rory Thornton and Adam Beard joined team-mate Bradley Davies on the region's roster of Welsh-capped second-rows.

Cardiff Blues consolidated their progress under Danny Wilson with a 50 per cent return in the PRO12. The highlight will have been their 35-17 success over Ospreys in the Easter double-header at the Millennium Stadium. Closer study of other wins shows that only two were achieved over teams finishing above them in the table: against Munster 24-23 in Cork and at home against Glasgow 23-19, both at the start of the season. Infrequent appearances, due to injury, by their two WRU dual-contract players Sam Warburton and Gareth Anscombe was an ongoing frustration. On a brighter note, younger players such as second-row Seb Davies and tight-head Dillon Lewis came to the fore, and became two more new caps on the South Seas tour. Progress was also made by back-rowers Ellis Jenkins and Josh Navidi, who along with hooker Kristian Dacey (one of the 'Geography Six' called up by the Lions) form part of the stalwart core available to Wilson.

European games gave cause for optimism. Five wins in a Challenge Cup pool containing Bath, Bristol and Pau saw the Blues into a quarter-final at Gloucester, where the eventual finalists were too strong (46-26). They also came second best to Stade (46-21) in a semi-final play-off for the last Champions Cup spot, so next season sees them again in the subsidiary competition with Sale, Lyon, and Toulouse, another former giant of the game seeking a return to loftier status.

Off the field, there are plans to develop the Arms Park as a covered multi-purpose arena. This led to a suggestion there were 'embryonic plans' for the WRU to take over the Blues franchise, at least on an interim basis. That was quickly shelved, but such an ownership change has gone ahead at Rodney Parade. Newport Gwent Dragons is no more, following a vote of Newport RFC shareholders at an EGM in May; from now on, it will simply be the Dragons. The eastern region has always struggled, and its playing record reflects the reduced budgets available to successive coaching groups. Now, the Welsh Rugby Union has moved from a 50 per cent holding to full ownership.

Last season's playing record illustrates the task ahead: a mere four league wins and eleventh place in the table. Not a single victory was achieved away from home all season, the few successes being against both Italian sides, plus Connacht and Edinburgh during the Autumn International window. Other successes were in the Challenge Cup over Brive and Worcester and the Russian side Enisei-STM. The Dragons have drawn the Russians again next season, along with Newcastle and Bordeaux.

Kingsley Jones has taken up a role with the WRU and is replaced as head coach by former Ireland hooker Bernard Jackman, most recently in the Top 14 with Grenoble. 'We will be taking the team out to the region at large and ensuring we are visible amongst all of the clubs in Gwent,' said the new man, in a statement of intent which will please supporters beyond the Newport area. The new arrangements will include national coach Warren Gatland helping out at training. Other plans include a hybrid pitch, which should be pleasing to co-tenants Newport County AFC.

There is still plenty of talent on the playing staff, including dual-contracted Tyler Morgan and Hallam Amos (the wing deserving an injury-free run), forwards Ollie Griffiths and Cory Hill, both first capped for Wales last season (the second-row being another of the Lions injury-cover call-ups) and the prodigal Gavin Henson back in Wales after some strong performances at Bristol.

It does not take a banking or accountancy qualification to deduce that financing the professional game in Wales is getting no easier. One influential regional board member is of the view that the nation can only realistically sustain two teams in the longer term, capable of punching their weight at the highest level. The long-awaited winning of a trophy by the Scarlets shows there is a good outlook on the domestic front playing-wise, but success on the tougher fields of European competition remains still some way off.

IRELAND: CON BRING THE TITLE BACK TO MUNSTER
by RUAIDHRI O'CONNOR

To add the Bateman (All Ireland) Cup to the bargain makes it a historic campaign for the Temple Hill club whose pre-eminence at the end of 2016-17 under coach Brian Hickey cannot be disputed

For the first time since 2010, the All Ireland League title resides outside of the capital after Cork Constitution finally ended the Leinster stranglehold on the trophy. Since they last won the competition, four different Dublin-based clubs have got their hands on the cup during an unprecedented period of dominance from the east coast.

From 1991 until 2011, only St Mary's had managed to get to the top as clubs from Munster and Ulster shared the spoils but a combination of economic and rugby factors contributed to a significant shift in recent years. While other giants of the early years of the competition have fallen far during that period, Cork Con have remained competitive in the face of circumstances.

To claim the title in a memorable final against Clontarf would have been particularly satisfying. The north Dublin club had attracted a host of players from Ireland's second city to their ranks and they played a role in their 2014 and 2016 league wins, so for Con to avenge their loss in last season's final will have been an enjoyable feeling.

To add the Bateman (All Ireland) Cup to the bargain makes it a historic campaign for the Temple Hill club whose pre-eminence at the end of 2016-17 under coach Brian Hickey cannot be disputed. Although Con finished the regular season in fourth, the quartet of semi-finalists had just a point to separate them after an 18-game campaign. It was the closest finish since the play-offs were reintroduced. UCD, the fifth-placed side, were 13 points off.

Lansdowne topped the table on points difference after finishing level with Clontarf and Young Munster on 58, with Con one back on 57, and the fourth-placed side were pitted against the long-term leaders away from home in their semi-final with 'Tarf hosting Young Munster in the other clash.

Both Munster clubs were affected by Munster A's presence in the British & Irish Cup final on the same weekend, but Con put their loss of contracted players to one side and knuckled down to their difficult task. In the end, they needed a late Tomás Quinlan penalty to prevent extra time and earn a 19-16 win that booked their place in the finale, back at the same venue but on the main pitch against Clontarf who had defeated the depleted Cookies 37-29 at Castle Avenue.

After Joey Carbery had dominated last season's run-in and gone on to earn an Ireland cap in the win over New Zealand within six months of the final, more eyes were on the lookout for another rising

FACING PAGE Cork Con receive the Division 1A trophy from IRFU president Stephen Hilditch after beating Clontarf in the final.

BELOW Clontarf's Mick McGrath, an Ireland Sevens international, powers past Con's Jason Higgins in the Division 1A final.

star and out-half Quinlan emerged as the frontrunner with a star turn in the final. A reliable kicker who also ran the game well for his team, he had been on the losing side to Clontarf a year previously but he and his team-mates gained their revenge in a 25-21 win at a sun-kissed Aviva Stadium.

Quinlan kicked 20 points in total, but it was far from plain sailing for the southern side who struggled at times with the holders' big ball carriers. Former Leinster back Mick McGrath in particular threatened to dominate the final early on with the physical winger causing the Con side all sorts of problems with his direct running and capacity to offload. The Ireland Sevens international added a score of his own before half-time, but the meticulous boot of Quinlan helped keep the Cork side in the game until they pounced for their only try, created by the pace of former Munster lock Brian Hayes who raced clear before feeding Rob Jermyn to score. A subsequent penalty and yellow card conceded by Sam Cronin gave the men from Munster a lead that Clontarf, try as they might, could never haul in, and the trophy went south.

'It's about time,' their captain Niall Kenneally said of the long-overdue success. 'I'm happy and relieved for the lads after all of the effort we put in. It's a long season.

'It wasn't a perfect final, but what a contest. Both teams gave it everything. The majority of us are amateur players, this is our lives and we give a lot of time and effort to it. These are the good days.'

Kenneally was voted the Ulster Bank League's Division 1A Player of the Year and after a starring role in the final Quinlan earned the Rising Star of the Year award. He was delighted to have put the memory of last year's final to bed.

'It is the complete opposite of what happened to us last year,' the out-half said. 'There was a lot of hurt taken onto the pitch and it showed there in the end in our defence; everyone stepped up individually and that allowed us to pull through.

'They kept coming at us in waves and we just wouldn't back down. Thankfully we did the job, which was an absolute relief to be honest.'

Despite having guided his team to every other available trophy, Hickey admitted that this was the prize Con most coveted after their long period without claiming the title. 'Really, if we were saying it was a great season even though we'd lost, I don't think it would have cut any ice with the players,' he said. 'This was the one we really wanted. At times we weren't even looking like getting into the top four.

'It's been an effort. We've had guys travelling. The likes of Gavin Duffy travelling to training sessions, Ger Sweeney is up the country the whole time, the way Munster players are coming back and buying in when they're released to us – particularly the academy players – you see it in all the teams in 1A.

'They know this is a very good standard and I think that's the most pleasing thing. A player who might play 20 minutes of a Friday night in the B&I Cup, they want to play with the club on the Saturday because they know the level it's at and they're with their own friends.'

Hickey claimed the Coach of the Year award to complete the picture of Con dominance at the end-of-year ceremony, but as they celebrated, at the other end of the table former Ireland coach Eddie O'Sullivan couldn't save 2011 winners Old Belvedere from the drop as they finished bottom of the division.

Buccaneers will replace them after topping the table in Division 1B in comprehensive fashion, winning 15 games out of 18 under former Connacht prop Brett Wilkinson who left the club at the end of a successful season to move to Hong Kong. The Midlanders finished 18 points clear of Naas and they were the only team promoted from the second tier as UL Bohemian were unable to unseat Limerick rivals Garryowen who gained a hard-fought 18-13 win in the Division 1B promotion play-off final.

At the bottom of Division 1B, Galwegians dropped down a level to be replaced by Banbridge who won Division 2A, while Greystones claimed the 2B title and Navan won 2C.

The season will be remembered as Cork Constitution's year, however, as they brought the Division 1A title back to its old permanent residence of Munster. The challenge now is for the storied Cork club to close the gap on the all-time list between themselves and Shannon, who remain out in front with nine titles. But the Limerick side are currently languishing in Division 1B and Con will want to make hay and add to their fifth title by keeping it on Leeside next season.

FRANCE: CLERMONT ARE THE BRIDES AT LAST

by **CHRIS THAU**

The final saw the perennial championship underachievers Clermont Auvergne outgun RC Toulon 22-16 to win their second Bouclier de Brennus from 14 finals

At the end of the regular season, the French Top 14 league table had a peculiar look about it, with the unfashionable La Rochelle club at the top with 85 points, and the multiple champions Stade Toulousain near the bottom in twelfth position, more than 30 points adrift – probably the lowest placing in the club's illustrious history. Below Toulouse opened the chasm of second division relegation, with Bayonne and Grenoble going down, to be replaced next season by Pro D2 league champions Oyonnax and SU Agen, the winners of the Pro D2 play-offs. Former French champions and 2012 European Challenge Cup winners Biarritz Olympique failed in their bid to return to the Top 14, leaving the Basque region, one of the most productive nurseries of French rugby, without representation in the elite division. However, now, with both Basque clubs Bayonne and Biarritz in the second division, the proposed merger to create a powerful mega-club in the region, rejected by the Bayonne membership a year ago, might gather enough support to go ahead.

By the end of the season the damaging effects of the ill-timed and badly managed proposed amalgamation of the Parisian clubs Stade Français and Racing 92 had somehow dissipated, with reigning champions Racing 92 regaining their killer touch to qualify for the Top 14 play-offs, and Stade Français missing the play-offs by a whisker, yet finishing as worthy winners of the European Challenge Cup. Thomas Savare, the Stade owner, stepped down, while the Heidelberg-born billionaire Hans-Peter Wild, the sponsor of the leading German professional club Heidelberger RK, took over, in itself a remarkable development that might well change the face of continental rugby. The new general manager of the club is former German international forward Robert Mohr, who played for Bourgoin and La Rochelle in France.

The Top 14 play-offs saw the rejuvenated Racing 92 knock out Montpellier 22-13, and Toulon, recovering their composure after a fairly uneven season, move into the semi-finals at the expense of Castres Olympique (26-22). In the semis, Clermont, who finished the regular season in the familiar position of runners-up, had the better of Racing 37-31 in a fast and furious game in which scrum half talisman Morgan Parra and his outside half partner Camille Lopez dominated with authority. In the other match, with the scores tied 15-all in the closing stages of a bruising encounter, Toulon's novice outside half Anthony Belleau produced a piece of magic to land a dropped goal to end La Rochelle's dreams of glory and steal the win 18-15. The final saw the perennial championship underachievers Clermont Auvergne outgun RC Toulon 22-16 to win their second Bouclier de Brennus (from 14 finals), a sweet and deserved revenge for their 28-17 mauling at the hands of Saracens in the European Champions Cup final a few weeks earlier.

As the domestic season was drawing to a close and the French coach Guy Novès announced the squad for the three-Test tour of South Africa, French rugby's officialdom got into overdrive trying to conclude the new agreement between the

LEFT Clermont Auvergne fans watch their team beat Toulon 22-16 at Stade de France to lift the 2016-17 Top 14 title.

French Federation (FFR) and the Ligue Nationale de Rugby (LNR), the body running the professional game in the country, regarding the availability of international players for squad training and preparations with the national team. The previous agreement which was approved in 2013 was due to expire at the end of the 2016-17 season. The federation, driven by its new dynamic president Bernard Laporte, is thought to have won the new round of negotiations with the professional clubs, as the international squad was expanded from 30 to 45 players and their availability from eight to ten weeks. It was a costly exercise, as the FFR contribution to the clubs has been increased by an additional 2.2 million euros, but as the outcome of the French tour to South Africa showed, it was a timely and much needed deal. The 3-0 whitewash in the series against the rejuvenated Springboks offered a clear statement of falling French standards, ending another rebuilding season by head coach Guy Novès, who has retained, just, the confidence of President Laporte.

The 2016-17 international season had started in November with a 52-8 walkover against a weak Samoa, followed a week later by a two-point defeat (25-23) at the hands of the Wallabies. The third match of the autumn series also resulted in a narrow loss for France, this time to New Zealand 24-19, but featured a display described by a reporter as 'the best French performance put on by a French side in close to ten years and … a throwback to the good old days of French flair'. France's Six Nations campaign ended with arguably the most bizarre match in living memory, when a combination of French gamesmanship and Welsh fatigue secured France an unexpected 20-18 win after 100 minutes of extraordinary rugby. The French lost to both England (19-16) and Ireland (19-9), but finished third thanks to a narrow 22-16 win over Scotland, a 40-18 defeat of Italy and the Welsh farce.

The June Test series between South Africa and France revealed the fundamental weaknesses of the French squad, as the visitors were consistently outplayed by the fired-up Springboks in all three Tests. It has to be said that the sorry state of affairs got laid bare by the fairly identical scorelines in the three matches – 37-14, 37-15 and 35-12 – regardless of personnel changes, promises and rhetoric. In fact, there is consensus in the French media that hardly any of the players who went to South Africa, with the exception of young Damian Penaud, have returned with their reputations enhanced. Coach Novès seemed to have found reasons for cautious optimism after the South African debacle, but the warning of Laporte sounded menacing: France must win three out of four Tests in November – New Zealand twice, South Africa and Japan – or else. Even more ominous sounded his comment about his former role as French coach and selector, which for the time being Novès has conveniently ignored.

ITALY: BLOWING COLD MORE OFTEN THAN HOT?

by CHRIS THAU

In the 2016-17 PRO12, between them the two Italian teams won eight of their 44 matches, with Benetton winning 19-3 against their Italian counterparts in the final clash of their campaign

The eighteenth season since the Five Nations Championship morphed into its six-country equivalent was remarkably eventful by any standard. And although the France v Wales game ended in a whirl of argument and recrimination, it was the match between England and Italy that will remain as the most controversial of the series. The innovative thinking of the Italian coaching team of Conor O'Shea, Mike Catt and Brendan Venter, who decided not to commit players to the breakdown after a tackle, produced a riddle that mystified the English players, who seemed unable to unravel the legal implications of the Italian action. This was somehow surprising because the tactic is virtually identical to the line-out ploy in which the defending team pulls back after the throw-in, refusing to create an offside line. The one-liner uttered by the French referee Romain Poite when prodded by James Haskell to explain what was happening has entered the realm of rugby folklore: 'Ask your coach, I am the referee,' he said. That prompted some television pundits, including former Scotland captain Andy Nicol, to put Poite forward as the man of the match.

Former England and Lions hooker Brian Moore, on duty as a television commentator, was astonished by the inability of the English players to adapt and react to what was by and large a simple question of the laws: 'These are professional players. They should know the laws. Very clever by the Italians,' he said during his live commentary. The reaction of the England coach Eddie Jones after the game did not help the matter: 'I am not happy with what happened today. That's not rugby,' he said, suggesting that the Italians had been somehow guilty of gamesmanship, which was obviously not the case. In fact, Italy's O'Shea was keen to make

the point after the match: 'We played within the laws of the game,' he said, explaining that they had approached the referee before the match to discuss the plan. Former England coach Clive Woodward praised the Italian approach: 'I totally support Italy and their use of their innovative and inspired tactics at Twickenham on Sunday. It was one of those rare moments in Test rugby that, as a former coach and player, make you sit bolt upright in your seat and think, "Wow, this is different, this is new. What on earth will England do next?"'

England eventually won the match, but the Italians left the field with their heads held high. This was Italy's sixth Test since the beginning of the season, which started ominously with a 68-10 hammering at the hands of New Zealand in Rome on 12 November. A week later they surprised the world and themselves with a laboured, yet valuable, 20-18 win (their first ever) against South Africa in Florence, only to finish the November Test window with a narrow 19-17 defeat at the hands of Tonga – a 'hot and cold' blueprint that seemed to have become a prototype of their international campaigns. The same could be said about the two Italian professional franchises, Benetton Treviso and Zebre of Parma, only that the 'cold' factor seemed to be more frequent.

In the 2016-17 PRO12, between them the two Italian teams won eight of their 44 matches, with Benetton winning 19-3 against their Italian counterparts in the final clash of their campaign. Treviso finished tenth and Zebre twelfth (last) in the Guinness PRO12, a place they have made almost their own since they joined the league at the beginning of the 2012-13 season. Beset by financial problems (about a million euros' deficit) and dwindling support, Zebre are about to follow in the footsteps of their predecessors Aironi of Viadana, pulled out by the Italian Federation at the end of the 2011-12 season. At the time of writing, the federation announced that a new, centrally funded franchise, also called Zebre, will replace the failed one next season, with the federation honouring the contracts of the players and staff.

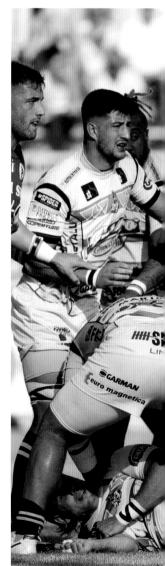

In the Six Nations Italy led Wales 7-3 at half-time to lose 33-7. Similarly they led England 10-5 at the break only to lose 36-15. Against France they were 16-11 down at half-time, with France winning 40-18 in the end, and so on. This pattern seemed to spread out to the summer tour, which started with an eminently forgettable 34-13 defeat by Scotland in Singapore, followed by a very promising performance in the 22-19 defeat at the hands of Fiji in Suva, and ended with arguably Italy's finest display against the Wallabies in Brisbane. With the visitors dominating the set-piece and the Australians leading by one point 28-27, two tries in the last five minutes gave the Wallabies the upper hand to secure a 40-27 win in an exciting match they could have easily lost. It is quite clear that O'Shea has identified the source of this infuriating inconsistency in the Italian development structure, having convinced the former IRFU technical director Steve Aboud to come to Italy to help him sort things out. 'They desperately want to succeed and they want to do it quickly. This is very good, but every project where you work with people it does take time to change minds, think in a different way. Players will need time to adapt,' explained Aboud in an interview.

In the absence of Sergio Parisse, left behind to rest after a hard season, it was new captain Francesco Minto, the Benetton flanker, who emphasised the objectives of the summer tour: 'At this stage in our development, I believe the quality of our game is more important than winning. That will come in due course.' All this has been taking place against a background of renewal, as O'Shea has been tinkering with the available personnel in an attempt to expand the

RIGHT Patarò Calvisano scrum half Fabio Semenzato launches the ball downfield over the oncoming Femi-CZ Rovigo forwards during the Italian championship final, which Calvisano won 43-29.

PAGE 141 Marcello Violi spins the ball out to the Zebre back line during the Italian side's 45-10 Good Friday defeat in Glasgow. Zebre won only three PRO12 games in finishing bottom of the 2016-17 table.

limited selection base of the Italian squad. With several veterans, including Parisse, Ghiraldini, Favaro, Cittadini, Zanni and McLean, unavailable to tour for a variety of reasons, there were nine uncapped players in the 44-strong enlarged squad summoned for the summer tour. The tour also offered Atkinson Coaching Ltd, the company retained by the Italian Federation until May 2020 to look after the strength and conditioning of the Italian players, the opportunity to commence working with the squad.

'I am proud of what the guys did today and throughout the tour,' said O'Shea after the Australian Test. 'Today's performance confirms the fact that, if we continue to make the necessary changes to our system, we will become very competitive in the seasons ahead. Now the boys have produced an incredible effort, but especially grew during those weeks: today we have created a great opportunity and we did it playing like Italy, focusing on our scrum that was brilliant this week, but also on the backs. I am sorry we have lost, but proud of what the team produced today on the field.'

The regular domestic season ended with Patarò Rugby Calvisano, coached by Massimo Brunello, at the top of the ten-strong Italian League, which they dominated, winning 17 out of 18 matches; last year's champions Femi-CZ Rugby Rovigo Delta finished third, and Petrarca Padova second. The play-offs final saw Calvisano, captained by hooker Gabriele Morelli, demolish Rovigo 43-29 at Pata Stadium 'San Michele' in Calvisano to lift their sixth championship title since the club was formed in 1970.

A Summary of the Season 2016-17

by TERRY COOPER

INTERNATIONAL RUGBY

NEW ZEALAND TO USA & EUROPE, NOVEMBER 2016

Opponents	Results
IRELAND (in Chicago)	L 29-40
ITALY	W 68-10
IRELAND	W 21-9
FRANCE	W 24-19

Played 4 Won 3 Lost 1

SOUTH AFRICA TO EUROPE, NOVEMBER 2016

Opponents	Results
Barbarians	D 31-31
ENGLAND	L 21-37
ITALY	L 18-20
WALES	L 13-27

Played 4 Drawn 1 Lost 3

AUSTRALIA TO EUROPE, NOVEMBER/DECEMBER 2016

Opponents	Results
WALES	W 32-8
SCOTLAND	W 23-22
FRANCE	W 25-23
French Barbarians	L 11-19
IRELAND	L 24-27
ENGLAND	L 21-37

Played 6 Won 3 Lost 3

ARGENTINA TO JAPAN & UK, NOVEMBER 2016

Opponents	Results
JAPAN	W 54-20
WALES	L 20-24
SCOTLAND	L 16-19
ENGLAND	L 14-27

Played 4 Won 1 Lost 3

BRITISH & IRISH LIONS TO NEW ZEALAND, JUNE/JULY 2017

Opponents	Results
Provincial Barbarians	W 13-7
Blues	L 16-22
Crusaders	W 12-3
Highlanders	L 22-23
Maori All Blacks	W 32-10
Chiefs	W 34-6
NEW ZEALAND	L 15-30
Hurricanes	D 31-31
NEW ZEALAND	W 24-21
NEW ZEALAND	D 15-15

Played 10 Won 5 Drawn 2 Lost 3

ENGLAND TO ARGENTINA, JUNE 2017

Opponents	Results
ARGENTINA	W 38–34
ARGENTINA	W 35-25

Played 2 Won 2

SCOTLAND TO SINGAPORE, AUSTRALIA & FIJI, JUNE 2017

Opponents	Results
ITALY	W 34–13
AUSTRALIA	W 24-19
FIJI	L 22-27

Played 3 Won 2 Lost 1

WALES TO TONGA & SAMOA, JUNE 2017

Opponents	Results
TONGA	W 24-6
SAMOA	W 19-17

Played 2 Won 2

IRELAND TO USA & JAPAN, JUNE 2017

Opponents	Results
USA	W 55–19
JAPAN	W 50–22
JAPAN	W 35-13

Played 3 Won 3

FRANCE TO SOUTH AFRICA, JUNE 2017

Opponents	Results
SOUTH AFRICA	L 14–37
SOUTH AFRICA	L 15–37
SOUTH AFRICA	L 12-35

Played 3 Lost 3

ITALY TO FIJI & AUSTRALIA, JUNE 2017

Opponents	Results
FIJI	L 19–22
AUSTRALIA	L 27-40

Played 2 Lost 2

OTHER INTERNATIONAL MATCHES 2016-17

New Zealand	37	Australia	10

(Third tie in Bledisloe Cup; see also The Rugby Championship)

Ireland	52	Canada	21
France	52	Samoa	8
England	58	Fiji	15
Wales	33	Japan	30
Scotland	43	Georgia	16
Italy	17	Tonga	19
Australia	37	Fiji	14
New Zealand	78	Samoa	0

RBS 6 NATIONS CHAMPIONSHIP 2017

Scotland	27	Ireland	22
England	19	France	16
Italy	7	Wales	33
Italy	10	Ireland	63
Wales	16	England	21
France	22	Scotland	16
Scotland	29	Wales	13
Ireland	19	France	9
England	36	Italy	15
Wales	22	Ireland	9
Italy	18	France	40
England	61	Scotland	21
Scotland	29	Italy	0
France	20	Wales	18
Ireland	13	England	9

	P	W	D	L	PD	BP	Pts
England	5	4	0	1	65	3	19
Ireland	5	3	0	2	49	2	14
France	5	3	0	2	17	2	14
Scotland	5	3	0	2	4	2	14
Wales	5	2	0	3	16	2	10
Italy	5	0	0	5	-151	0	0

WOMEN'S SIX NATIONS 2017

Scotland	15	Ireland	22
Italy	8	Wales	20
England	26	France	13
Wales	0	England	63
France	55	Scotland	0
Italy	3	Ireland	27
Scotland	15	Wales	14
England	29	Italy	15
Ireland	13	France	10
Wales	7	Ireland	12
England	64	Scotland	0
Italy	5	France	28
Scotland	14	Italy	12
Ireland	7	England	34
France	39	Wales	19

	P	W	D	L	PD	BP	Pts
England	5	5	0	0	181	4	27
Ireland	5	4	0	1	12	2	18
France	5	3	0	2	82	4	16
Scotland	5	2	0	3	-123	1	9
Wales	5	1	0	4	-77	2	6
Italy	5	0	0	5	-75	1	1

UNDER 20 SIX NATIONS 2017

Italy	5	Wales	27
Scotland	19	Ireland	20
England	59	France	17
Italy	26	Ireland	27
Wales	21	England	37
France	36	Scotland	8
England	46	Italy	0
Ireland	27	France	22
Scotland	34	Wales	65
Italy	13	France	18
England	33	Scotland	5
Wales	41	Ireland	27
Ireland	10	England	14
Scotland	38	Italy	17
France	40	Wales	20

	P	W	D	L	PD	BP	Pts
England	5	5	0	0	136	4	27
France	5	3	0	2	6	3	15
Wales	5	3	0	2	31	2	14
Ireland	5	3	0	2	-11	1	13
Scotland	5	1	0	4	-67	3	7
Italy	5	0	0	5	-95	2	2

WORLD RUGBY PACIFIC NATIONS CUP 2017

Fiji	23	Tonga	18
Fiji	26	Samoa	16
Samoa	30	Tonga	10
Tonga	30	Samoa	26
Tonga	10	Fiji	14
Samoa	16	Fiji	38

Champions: Fiji

WORLD RUGBY NATIONS CUP 2017

(Held in June in Montevideo)

Namibia	13	Spain	15
Argentina XV	38	Russia	39
Uruguay	30	Emerging Italy	21
Namibia	38	Emerging Italy	22
Argentina XV	37	Spain	5
Uruguay	32	Russia	29
Namibia	10	Russia	31
Argentina XV	15	Emerging Italy	10
Uruguay	24	Spain	14

Champions: Uruguay

WORLD RUGBY U20 CHAMPIONSHIP 2017

(Held in May/June in Georgia)

Third-place Play-off

South Africa	37	France	15

Final

New Zealand	64	England	17

For business.
For family.
For life.

Wealth is made of much more than money. It is realising hopes and dreams, passions and partnerships. At Arbuthnot Latham we strive to see beyond the obvious to help you achieve what really matters.

t: 020 7012 2500   arbuthnotlatham.co.t

RUGBY EUROPE U18 CHAMPIONSHIP 2017

(Held in April in Brittany)
Third-place Play-off
Portugal 16 Japan 22

Final
France 36 Georgia 18

THE RUGBY CHAMPIONSHIP 2016

Australia 8 New Zealand 42
(Also first tie in Bledisloe Cup)
South Africa 30 Argentina 23
New Zealand 29 Australia 9
(Also second tie in Bledisloe Cup)
Argentina 26 South Africa 24
New Zealand 57 Argentina 22
Australia 23 South Africa 17
New Zealand 41 South Africa 13
Australia 36 Argentina 20
South Africa 18 Australia 10
Argentina 17 New Zealand 36
South Africa 15 New Zealand 57
Argentina 21 Australia 33

	P	W	D	L	PD	BP	Pts
New Zealand	6	6	0	0	178	6	30
Australia	6	3	0	3	-28	1	13
South Africa	6	2	0	4	-63	2	10
Argentina	6	1	0	5	-87	1	5

WOMEN'S RUGBY WORLD CUP 2017

Pool A
	P	W	D	L	PD	BP	Pts
New Zealand	3	3	0	0	196	3	15
Canada	3	2	0	1	70	1	9
Wales	3	1	0	2	-23	1	5
Hong Kong	3	0	0	3	-243	0	0

Pool B
	P	W	D	L	PD	BP	Pts
England	3	3	0	0	115	3	15
USA	3	2	0	1	34	3	11
Spain	3	1	0	2	-80	0	4
Italy	3	0	0	3	-69	0	0

Pool C
	P	W	D	L	PD	BP	Pts
France	3	3	0	0	122	2	14
Ireland	3	2	0	1	-4	0	8
Australia	3	1	0	2	-36	2	6
Japan	3	0	0	3	-82	0	0

Semi-finals
New Zealand 45 USA 12
England 20 France 3

Third-place Play-off
France 31 USA 23

Final
England 32 New Zealand 41

HSBC WORLD RUGBY SEVENS SERIES FINALS 2016-17

Dubai
Fiji 14 South Africa 26

South Africa (Cape Town)
South Africa 17 England 19

New Zealand (Wellington)
Fiji 5 South Africa 26

Australia (Sydney)
England 14 South Africa 29

USA (Las Vegas)
South Africa 19 Fiji 12

Canada (Vancouver)
South Africa 7 England 19

Hong Kong
South Africa 0 Fiji 22

Singapore
USA 19 Canada 26

France (Paris)
Scotland 5 South Africa 15

England (Twickenham)
Scotland 12 England 7
Champions: South Africa

HSBC WORLD RUGBY WOMEN'S SEVENS SERIES FINALS 2016-17

Dubai
New Zealand 17 Australia 5

Australia (Sydney)
Canada 21 USA 17

USA (Las Vegas)
New Zealand 28 Australia 5

Japan (Kitakyushu)
New Zealand 17 Canada 14

Canada (Langford)
New Zealand 17 Canada 7

France (Clermont-Ferrand)
New Zealand 22 Australia 7
Champions: New Zealand

CLUB, COUNTY AND DIVISIONAL RUGBY

ENGLAND

Aviva Premiership

	P	W	D	L	F	A	BP	Pts
Wasps	22	17	1	4	693	502	14	84
Exeter	22	15	3	4	667	452	18	84
Saracens	22	16	1	5	579	345	11	77
Leicester	22	14	0	8	567	445	10	66
Bath	22	12	0	10	486	440	11	59
Harlequins	22	11	0	11	532	526	8	52
Northampton	22	10	0	12	476	490	12	52
Newcastle	22	10	0	12	430	581	9	49
Gloucester	22	7	2	13	533	537	14	46
Sale	22	7	1	14	471	595	10	40
Worcester	22	5	2	15	466	662	9	33
Bristol	22	3	0	19	382	707	8	20

Relegated: Bristol

Aviva Premiership Play-offs
Semi-finals
Exeter	18	Saracens	16
Wasps	21	Leicester	20

Final
Wasps	20	Exeter	23

Greene King IPA Championship Play-offs
Semi-finals (1st leg)
Ealing Trailfinders	16	Y'shire Carnegie	34
Doncaster Knights	3	London Irish	35

Semi-finals (2nd leg)
Y'shire Carnegie	18	Ealing Trailfinders	20
London Irish	39	Doncaster Knights	22

Final
Y'shire Carnegie	18	London Irish	29
London Irish	55	Y'shire Carnegie	48

Promoted to Premiership: London Irish

National Leagues
National 1 Champions: Hartpury College
Runners-up: Plymouth Albion
National 2 (S) Champions: Bishop's Stortford
Runners-up: Old Elthamians
National 2 (N) Champions: Caldy
Runners-up: Sale

National 2 N & S Runners-up Play-off
Sale	14	Old Elthamians	19

RFU Knockout Trophies Finals
Intermediate Cup
West Leeds	35	Charlton Park	26
Senior Vase
| Farnham | 37 | Droitwich | 15 |
Junior Vase
| Goole | 31 | Spartans | 24 |

Oxbridge University Matches
Varsity Match
Oxford	18	Cambridge	23
Women's Varsity Match
| Oxford | 3 | Cambridge | 0 |

Bill Beaumont Senior Men's County Championship
Division 1 Final
Lancashire	19	Cornwall	8
Division 2 Final
| Leicestershire | 39 | Hampshire | 7 |
Division 3 Final
| Oxfordshire | 29 | Sussex | 29 |

(Oxfordshire win on try count)

Gill Burns Women's County Championship
Division 1 Final
Lancashire	25	Surrey	13
Division 2 Final
| Leicestershire | 32 | Essex | 29 |

Jason Leonard U20 County Championship
Division 1 Final
Yorkshire	14	Durham	7
Division 2 Final
| Cheshire | 29 | Dorset & Wilts | 20 |

BUCS Competitions
Super Rugby Champions: Hartpury College
Men's Championship Winners: Hartpury College
Women's Championship Winners: Edinburgh U

Inter-Services Championship
Royal Air Force	16	Royal Navy	14
Army	35	Royal Air Force	14
Army	29	Royal Navy	20
Champions: Army

Rosslyn Park HSBC National Schools Sevens
Cup Winners: Cranleigh
Vase Winners: St John's Leatherhead
Girls Winners: Amman Valley School
Girls AASE Winners: Hartpury College
Colts Winners: Wellington College
U14 Winners: Wimbledon College

NatWest Schools Cup and Vase Finals
U18 Champions Trophy Winners: Tonbridge
U18 Cup Winners: Warwick School
U18 Vase Winners: Trent College
U15 Cup Winners: Wellington College
U15 Vase Winners: The Thomas Hardye School

Women's Premiership

	P	W	D	L	F	A	BP	Pts
Bristol	14	12	0	2	524	188	12	60
Lichfield	14	12	0	2	462	211	11	59
Aylesford Bulls	14	10	0	4	451	229	9	49
Saracens	14	9	0	5	400	242	9	45
Worcester	14	6	0	8	354	374	7	31
Richmond	14	3	0	11	214	488	5	17
Wasps	14	2	0	12	229	604	5	13
DMP Sharks	14	2	0	12	200	498	4	12

Women's Premiership Play-off Final
Aylesford Bulls	17	Bristol	8

Women's Cup Final
Aylesford Bulls	37	Bristol	0

SCOTLAND

BT Cup Final
Melrose   23   Ayr   18

BT Shield Final
Murrayfield Wand'rs   28   Carrick   41

BT Bowl Final
Blairgowrie   23   Portobello   33

Scottish Sevens Winners
Peebles: Melrose
Gala: Watsonians
Melrose: Harlequins
Hawick: Gala
Berwick: Jed-Forest
Langholm: Selkirk
Kelso: Watsonians
Earlston: Gala
Selkirk: Melrose
Jed-Forest: Watsonians
Kings of the Sevens: Watsonians

BT Premiership

	P	W	D	L	F	A	BP	Pts
Melrose	18	16	0	2	579	285	14	78
Ayr	18	15	0	3	598	369	14	74
Glasgow Hawks	18	11	0	7	560	456	13	57
Currie	18	10	0	8	531	456	13	53
Heriot's	18	10	1	7	443	327	10	52
Watsonians	18	7	0	11	420	534	9	37
Boroughmuir	18	5	0	13	442	588	12	32
Stirling County	18	6	0	12	372	481	6	30
Hawick	18	5	1	12	364	565	8	30
Gala	18	4	0	14	371	619	7	23

BT Premiership Play-off Final
Melrose   8   Ayr   12

BT National League Division 1

	P	W	D	L	F	A	BP	Pts
Marr	22	21	0	1	901	323	18	102
Edinburgh Acads	22	19	0	3	748	326	22	98
Jed-Forest	22	14	0	8	742	590	15	71
Dundee HSFP	22	13	0	9	697	629	13	65
Falkirk	22	13	0	9	610	472	12	64
Selkirk	22	11	0	11	574	565	17	61
GHA	22	11	0	11	604	668	12	56
Stewart's Melville	22	9	0	13	440	605	11	47
Musselburgh	22	8	0	14	571	747	12	44
Aberdeen GS	22	6	0	16	511	724	16	40
Hamilton	22	4	0	18	472	868	12	28
Howe of Fife	22	3	0	19	462	815	11	22

BT Premiership-National 1 Play-off
Edinburgh Acads   20   Hawick   23

BT National League Division 2
Champions: Cartha Queens Park

BT Women's Premier League
Champions: Murrayfield Wanderers

BT Women's National League Division 1
Champions: Watsonians

Sarah Beaney Cup Final
Murrayfield Wand'rs   23   Hillhead Jordanhill 26

WALES

National Cup
Semi-finals
Pontypridd   42   Cross Keys   37
RGC 1404   26   Merthyr   20

Final
Pontypridd   11   RGC 1404   15

National Plate Final
Penallta   16   Ystalyfera   16
(Penallta win on try count)

National Bowl Final
Amman United   43   Caerphilly   31

Principality Premiership

	P	W	D	L	F	A	BP	Pts
Aberavon	15	11	1	3	475	277	9	55
Bedwas	15	10	1	4	377	269	10	52
Merthyr	15	10	0	5	442	321	11	51
RGC 1404	15	10	1	4	429	281	6	48
Pontypridd	15	10	0	5	389	371	7	47
C'marthen Quins	15	9	1	5	384	305	9	47
Llandovery	15	8	1	6	416	287	9	43
Ebbw Vale	15	9	0	6	354	311	6	42
Cardiff	15	7	0	8	325	314	9	37
Newport	15	7	0	8	291	339	5	33
Llanelli	15	6	1	8	291	367	6	32
Cross Keys	15	7	0	8	298	301	3	31
Bridgend	15	4	0	11	232	332	6	22
Neath	15	4	0	11	254	464	3	19
Bargoed	15	3	0	12	194	391	4	16
Swansea	15	2	0	13	237	458	5	13

National Championship

	P	W	D	L	F	A	BP	Pts
Pontypool	22	21	0	1	805	279	14	98
Narberth	22	17	0	5	649	362	13	81
Tata Steel	22	14	0	8	578	451	14	70
Beddau	22	14	0	8	535	397	14	70
N'castle Emlyn	22	10	1	11	411	504	12	54
Cardiff Met	22	10	0	12	435	562	6	46
Newbridge	22	9	0	13	403	534	9	45
Glynneath	22	10	0	12	339	488	4	44
Bedlinog	22	8	1	13	407	440	10	44
Skewen	22	8	1	13	314	418	7	41
The Wanderers	22	7	1	14	405	490	11	41
Dunvant	22	2	0	20	434	790	8	16

National Leagues
Division 1 East Champions: Rhydyfelin
Division 1 East Central Champions: Treorchy
Division 1 West Champions: Kidwelly
Division 1 West Central Champions: Trebanos
Division 1 North Champions: Pwllheli
Division 2 East Champions: Croesyceiliog
Division 2 East Central Champions: Dinas Powys
Division 2 West Champions: Tenby United
Division 2 West Central Champions: Tondu
Division 2 North Champions: Llangefni

Women's Premier Division
Champions: Swansea

Women's Super Cup Final
Swansea   23   Caernarfon   20

IRELAND

Ulster Bank League Division 1A

	P	W	D	L	F	A	BP	Pts
Lansdowne	18	11	1	6	503	332	12	58
Clontarf	18	11	0	7	414	272	14	58
Young Munster	18	11	0	7	418	357	14	58
Cork Constitution	18	13	0	5	386	295	5	57
UCD	18	8	1	9	368	408	10	44
Dublin University	18	9	0	9	315	413	3	39
St Mary's College	18	7	0	11	391	456	10	38
Terenure College	18	6	1	11	338	380	10	36
Garryowen	18	7	0	11	325	442	7	35
Old Belvedere	18	5	1	12	279	382	6	28

Ulster Bank League Division 1A Final
Clontarf 21 Cork Constitution 25

Ulster Bank League Division 1B

	P	W	D	L	F	A	BP	Pts
Buccaneers	18	15	1	2	517	308	10	72
Naas	18	11	0	7	368	285	10	54
UL Bohemian	18	11	0	7	406	395	8	52
Old Wesley	18	10	2	6	415	413	7	51
UCC	18	9	0	9	323	347	8	44
Ballymena	18	7	1	10	346	406	8	38
Ballynahinch	18	7	0	11	367	429	9	37
Shannon	18	6	1	11	303	363	10	36
Dolphin	18	8	0	10	293	380	2	34
Galwegians	18	3	1	14	378	390	14	28

Ulster Bank League Division 2A
Champions: Banbridge

Ulster Bank League Division 2B
Champions: Greystones

Ulster Bank League Division 2C
Champions: Navan

Round Robin
Clonmel	10	Ballina	6
Omagh	17	Malahide	26
Ballina	7	Omagh	17
Malahide	34	Clonmel	9
Ballina	38	Malahide	46
Omagh	25	Clonmel	13

Winners: Malahide

Ulster Bank All Ireland Bateman Cup Final
Cork Constitution 18 Old Belvedere 13

Ulster Bank All Ireland Junior Cup Final
Ashbourne 22 Enniscorthy 20

Fraser McMullen Cup Final
Lansdowne 9 Navan 22

Women's All Ireland League Division 1 Final
UL Bohemian 10 Old Belvedere 3

Women's All Ireland Cup Final
Blackrock 17 UL Bohemian 26

GUINNESS PRO12 2016-17

	P	W	D	L	F	A	BP	Pts
Munster	22	19	0	3	602	316	10	86
Leinster	22	18	0	4	674	390	13	85
Scarlets	22	17	0	5	537	359	9	77
Ospreys	22	14	0	8	556	360	13	69
Ulster	22	14	1	7	521	371	10	68
Glasgow	22	11	0	11	540	464	14	58
Cardiff	22	11	1	10	508	498	7	53
Connacht	22	9	0	13	413	498	8	44
Edinburgh	22	6	0	16	400	491	7	31
Treviso	22	5	0	17	316	664	3	23
Dragons	22	4	0	18	368	569	7	23
Zebre	22	3	0	19	318	773	7	19

Guinness PRO12 Play-offs
Semi-finals
Leinster	15	Scarlets	27
Munster	23	Ospreys	3

Final
Munster 22 Scarlets 46

ANGLO-WELSH CUP 2016-17

Semi-finals
Saracens	10	Leicester	32
Exeter	24	Harlequins	7

Final
Exeter 12 Leicester 16

BRITISH & IRISH CUP 2016-17

Semi-finals
Munster A	25	Ealing Trailfinders	9
London Irish	17	Jersey	25

Final
Munster A 29 Jersey 28

FRANCE

'Top 14' 2016-17 Play-offs
Semi-finals
La Rochelle	15	Toulon	18
Clermont Auvergne	37	Racing 92	31

Final
Clermont Auvergne 22 Toulon 16

ITALY

Campionato Italiano d'Eccellenza 2016-17 Play-offs
Semi-finals (1st leg)
Rovigo	33	Petrarca	18
Viadana	18	Calvisano	12

Semi-finals (2nd leg)
Calvisano	47	Viadana	17
Petrarca	12	Rovigo	28

Final
Calvisano 43 Rovigo 29

EUROPEAN RUGBY CHAMPIONS CUP 2016-17

Quarter-finals

Clermont Auvergne	29	Toulon	9
Leinster	32	Wasps	17
Saracens	38	Glasgow	13
Munster	41	Toulouse	16

Semi-finals

Clermont Auvergne	27	Leinster	22
Munster	10	Saracens	26

Final

Clermont Auvergne	17	Saracens	28

EUROPEAN RUGBY CHALLENGE CUP 2016-17

Quarter-finals

Ospreys	21	Stade Français	25
Bath	34	Brive	20
Edinburgh	22	La Rochelle	32
Gloucester	46	Cardiff	26

Semi-finals

Stade Français	28	Bath	25
La Rochelle	14	Gloucester	16

Final

Gloucester	17	Stade Français	25

NEW ZEALAND

Mitre 10 Cup Premiership Final 2016

Canterbury	43	Tasman	27

Mitre 10 Cup Championship Final 2016

Otago	14	North Harbour	17

Heartland Champions 2016
Meads Cup: Wanganui
Lochore Cup: North Otago

Ranfurly Shield holders: Canterbury

SOUTH AFRICA

Currie Cup 2016
Final

Cheetahs	36	Blue Bulls	16

SUPER RUGBY 2017

	P	W	D	L	F	A	BP	Pts
Lions	**15**	**14**	**0**	**1**	**590**	**268**	**9**	**65**
Crusaders	**15**	**14**	**0**	**1**	**544**	**303**	**7**	**63**
Stormers	**15**	**10**	**0**	**5**	**490**	**436**	**3**	**43**
Brumbies	**15**	**6**	**0**	**8**	**315**	**279**	**10**	**34**
Hurricanes	*15*	*12*	*0*	*3*	*596*	*272*	*10*	*58*
Chiefs	*15*	*12*	*1*	*2*	*433*	*292*	*7*	*57*
Highlanders	*15*	*11*	*0*	*4*	*488*	*308*	*7*	*51*
Sharks	*15*	*9*	*1*	*5*	*392*	*323*	*4*	*42*
Blues	15	7	1	7	425	391	7	37
Jaguares	15	7	0	8	408	386	5	33
Southern Kings	15	6	0	9	391	470	4	28
Force	15	6	0	9	313	404	1	26
Cheetahs	15	4	0	11	395	551	5	21
Reds	15	4	0	11	321	479	5	21
Bulls	15	4	0	11	339	459	4	20
Waratahs	15	4	0	11	396	522	3	19
Sunwolves	15	2	0	13	315	671	4	12
Rebels	15	1	1	13	236	569	3	9

Quarter-finals

Brumbies	16	Hurricanes	35
Crusaders	17	Highlanders	0
Lions	23	Sharks	21
Stormers	11	Chiefs	17

Semi-finals

Crusaders	27	Chiefs	13
Lions	44	Hurricanes	29

Final

Lions	17	Crusaders	25

Key
Lions: Conference winners
Hurricanes: Wild Card teams

The table is for guidance only. The eight Super Rugby play-off places are decided on a conference/regional basis, with the four Conference winners making up positions one to four. The Wild Card teams, three from NZ/Aus and one from South Africa, are the next best teams and make up positions five to eight.

BARBARIANS

Opponents	Results
South Africa XV	D 31–31
Czech Republic	W 71–0
Fiji XV	W 40–7
England XV	L 14–28
Ulster	W 43–28

Played 5 Won 3 Drawn 1 Lost 1

SARACENS SPORT FOUNDATION

PREVIEW OF THE SEASON 2017-18

Key Players

selected by IAN ROBERTSON

ENGLAND

ANTHONY WATSON
Bath
Born: 26 February 1994
Height: 6ft 1in Weight: 15st 1lb
Wing/full back – 26 caps (+3 Lions)
1st cap v New Zealand 2014

MAKO VUNIPOLA
Saracens
Born: 14 January 1991
Height: 5ft 11ins Weight: 19st
Prop – 42 caps (+6 Lions)
1st cap v Fiji 2012

SCOTLAND

TOMMY SEYMOUR
Glasgow
Born: 1 July 1988
Height: 6ft Weight: 14st 11lbs
Wing – 36 caps
1st cap v South Africa 2013

JOHN HARDIE
Edinburgh
Born: 27 July 1988
Height: 6ft Weight: 16st 3lbs
Back-row – 16 caps
1st cap v Italy 2015

WALES

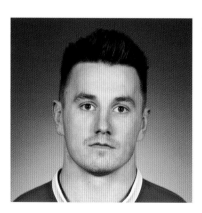

JONATHAN DAVIES
Scarlets
Born: 5 April 1988
Height: 6ft 1in Weight: 16st 5lbs
Centre – 64 caps (+6 Lions)
1st cap v Canada 2009

TAULUPE FALETAU
Bath
Born: 12 November 1990
Height: 6ft 2ins Weight: 17st 2lbs
Back-row – 66 caps (+4 Lions)
1st cap v Barbarians 2011

Six Nations Championship

IRELAND

ROBBIE HENSHAW
Leinster
Born: 12 June 1993
Height: 6ft 3ins Weight: 16st 3lbs
Centre – 29 caps
1st cap v USA 2013

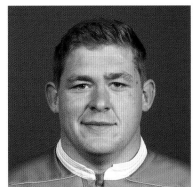

TADHG FURLONG
Leinster
Born: 14 November 1992
Height: 6ft 1in Weight: 19st 11lbs
Prop – 16 caps (+3 Lions)
1st cap v Wales 2015

FRANCE

CAMILLE LOPEZ
Clermont Auvergne
Born: 3 April 1989
Height: 5ft 9ins Weight: 13st 12lbs
Fly half – 16 caps
1st cap v New Zealand 2013

LOUIS PICAMOLES
Montpellier
Born: 5 February 1986
Height: 6ft 4ins Weight: 18st 8lbs
Back-row – 65 caps
1st cap v Ireland 2008

ITALY

MICHELE CAMPAGNARO
Exeter
Born: 13 March 1993
Height: 6ft Weight: 14st 11lbs
Centre – 32 caps
1st cap v Fiji 2013

FRANCESCO MINTO
Treviso
Born: 20 May 1987
Height: 6ft 4ins Weight: 16st 11lbs
Back-row – 36 caps
1st cap v New Zealand 2012

Fixtures 2017-18

AUGUST 2017

Sat. 19th	AUSTRALIA v NZ (TRC/BC)
	SA v ARGENTINA (TRC)
Thu. 24th to	
Sat. 26th	BT Scottish Nat Lge Cup (1)
Sat. 26th	NZ v AUSTRALIA (TRC/BC)
	ARGENTINA v SA (TRC)
	Welsh Principality Premiership (1)

SEPTEMBER 2017

Fri. 1st and	
Sat. 2nd	Guinness PRO14 (1)
	GK IPA Championship (1)
Fri. 1st to	
Sun. 3rd	Aviva English Premiership (1)
Sat. 2nd	English National Leagues
	BT Scottish Premiership (1)
	BT Scottish National Leagues
	Welsh Principality Premiership (2)
	Welsh National Championship
	Welsh National Leagues
Mon. 3rd	Aviva 'A' League
Fri 8th and	
Sat. 9th	Guinness PRO14 (2)
Fri. 8th to	
Sun. 10th	Aviva English Premiership (2)
	GK IPA Championship (2)
Sat. 9th	NZ v ARGENTINA (TRC)
	AUSTRALIA v SA (TRC)
	English National Leagues
	BT Scottish Premiership (2)
	BT Scottish National Leagues
	Welsh Principality Premiership (3)
	Welsh National Championship
	Welsh National Leagues
Mon. 11th	Aviva 'A' League
Fri. 15th	
to Sun. 17th	Guinness PRO14 (3)
	Aviva English Premiership (3)
	GK IPA Championship (3)
Sat. 16th	NZ v SA (TRC/FC)
	AUSTRALIA v ARGENTINA (TRC)
	English National Leagues
	BT Scottish Premiership (3)
	BT Scottish National Leagues
	Welsh Principality Premiership (4)
	Welsh National Championship
	Welsh National Leagues
	Welsh National Bowl (1)
	Ulster Bank Irish Leagues
Fri. 22nd and	
Sat 23rd	Guinness PRO14 (4)
	Ulster Bank Irish Leagues
Fri. 22nd to	
Sun. 24th	Aviva English Premiership (4)

Sat. 23rd	English National Leagues
	BT Scottish Premiership (4)
	BT Scottish National Leagues
	Welsh Principality Premiership (5)
	Welsh National Championship
	Welsh National Leagues
Sat. 23rd and	
Sun. 24th	GK IPA Championship (4)
Mon. 25th	Aviva 'A' League
Fri. 29th and	
Sat. 30th	Guinness PRO14 (5)
Fri. 29th to	
Sun. 1st Oct.	Aviva English Premiership (5)
	GK IPA Championship (5)
Sat. 30th	ARGENTINA v NZ (TRC)
	SA v AUSTRALIA (TRC/MCP)
	English National Leagues
	BT Scottish Premiership (5)
	BT Scottish National Leagues
	Welsh Principality Premiership (6)
	Welsh National Championship
	Welsh National Leagues
	Ulster Bank Irish Leagues

OCTOBER 2017

Mon. 2nd	Aviva 'A' League
Fri. 6th and	
Sat. 7th	Guinness PRO14 (6)
	Ulster Bank Irish Leagues
Fri. 6th to	
Sun. 8th	Aviva English Premiership (6)
Sat. 7th	SA v NZ (TRC/FC)
	ARGENTINA v AUSTRALIA
	(TRC – Twickenham)
	English National Leagues
	BT Scottish Premiership (6)
	BT Scottish National League
	Welsh Principality Premiership (7)
	Welsh National Championship
	Welsh National Plate (1)
Sat. 7th and	
Sun. 8th	GK IPA Championship (6)
Thu. 12th to	
Sun. 15th	European Champions Cup (1)
	European Challenge Cup (1)
Fri. 13th to	
Sun. 15th	British & Irish Cup (1)
Sat. 14th	English National Leagues
	BT Scottish Premiership (7)
	BT Scottish National Leagues
	Welsh National Championship
	Welsh National Leagues
Thu. 19th to	
Sun. 22nd	European Champions Cup (2)
	European Challenge Cup (2)

Fri. 20th to
Sun. 22nd   British & Irish Cup (2)
Sat. 21st   NZ v AUSTRALIA (BC)
               English National Leagues
               BT Scottish Premiership (8)
               BT Scottish National Leagues
               Welsh National Championship
               Welsh National Leagues
Mon. 23rd   Aviva 'A' League
Fri. 27th and
Sat. 28th   Guinness PRO14 (7)
               Ulster Bank Irish Leagues

Fri. 27th to
Sun. 29th   Aviva English Premiership (7)
               GK IPA Championship (7)
Sat. 28th   English National Leagues
               BT Scottish Premiership (9)
               BT Scottish National Leagues
               Welsh Principality Premiership (8)
               Welsh National Championship

NOVEMBER 2017

Fri. 3rd and
Sat. 4th   Guinness PRO14 (8)
Fri. 3rd to
Sun. 5th   Anglo-Welsh Cup (1)
Sat. 4th   Barbarians v NZ (Twickenham)
               English National Leagues
               BT Scottish Premiership (10)
               BT Scottish National Leagues
               Welsh Principality Premiership (9)
               Welsh National Championship
               Welsh National Leagues
               Ulster Bank Irish Leagues
Fri. 10th and
Sat. 11th   Ulster Bank Irish Leagues
Fri. 10th to
Sun. 12th   GK IPA Championship (8)
               Anglo-Welsh Cup (2)
Sat. 11th   ENGLAND v ARGENTINA
               FRANCE v NZ
               WALES v AUSTRALIA
               SCOTLAND v SAMOA
               IRELAND v SA
               ITALY v FIJI
               English National Leagues
               Welsh Principality Premiership (10)
               Welsh National Championship
               Welsh National Leagues
Fri. 17th to
Sun. 19th   Aviva English Premiership (8)
               GK IPA Championship (9)
               Anglo-Welsh Cup (1)*
Sat. 18th   ENGLAND v AUSTRALIA
               WALES v GEORGIA
               SCOTLAND v NZ
               IRELAND v FIJI
               FRANCE v SA
               ITALY v ARGENTINA
               BT Scottish Cup (1)
               BT Scottish Nat Lge Cup (2)
               Welsh Principality Premiership (11)
               Welsh National Leagues

Fri. 24th and
Sat. 25th   GK IPA Championship (10)
               Ulster Bank Irish Leagues
Fri. 24th to
Sun. 26th   Guinness PRO14 (9)
               Aviva English Premiership (9)
Sat. 25th   ENGLAND v SAMOA
               SCOTLAND v AUSTRALIA
               IRELAND v ARGENTINA
               WALES v NZ
               FRANCE v JAPAN
               ITALY v SA
               English National Leagues
               Welsh Principality Premiership (12)
Mon. 27th   Aviva 'A' League

DECEMBER 2017

Fri. 1st and
Sat. 2nd   HSBC 7s World Series (Dubai)
               Guinness PRO14 (10)
Fri. 1st to
Sun. 3rd   Aviva English Premiership (10)
               GK IPA Championship (11)
Sat. 2nd   WALES v SA
               English National Leagues
               BT Scottish Premiership (11)
               BT Scottish National Leagues
               Welsh Principality Premiership (13)
               Ulster Bank Irish Leagues
Thu. 7th   OU Women v CU Women 11:30
               OU v CU 14:30
                  (both Twickenham)
Thu. 7th to
Sun. 10th   European Champions Cup (3)
               European Challenge Cup (3)
Fri. 8th to
Sun. 10th   British & Irish Cup (3)
Sat. 9th   English National Leagues
               BT Scottish Premiership (12)
               BT Scottish National Leagues
               Welsh National Championship
Sat. 9th and
Sun. 10th   HSBC 7s World Series (Cape T'n)
Thu. 14th to
Sun. 17th   European Champions Cup (4)
               European Challenge Cup (4)
Fri. 15th to
Sun. 17th   British & Irish Cup (4)
Sat. 16th   English National Leagues
               BT Scottish Premiership (13)
               BT Scottish National Leagues
               Welsh National Championship
               Welsh National Leagues
Mon. 18th   Aviva 'A' League
Fri. 22nd and
Sat. 23rd   GK IPA Championship (12)
Fri. 22nd to
Sun. 24th   Aviva English Premiership (11)
Sat. 23rd   English National Leagues
               Welsh Principality Premiership (14)
Sat. 23rd and
Tue. 26th   Guinness PRO14 (11)

Fri. 29th to		
Sun. 31st	Aviva English Premiership (12)	
	GK IPA Championship (13)	
Sat. 30th	Welsh Principality Premiership (15)	
	Welsh National Championship	
	Welsh National Leagues	
Sat. 30th to		
Mon. 1st Jan.	Guinness PRO14 (12)	

JANUARY 2018

Mon. 1st	Aviva 'A' League
Fri. 5th and	
Sat. 6th	Ulster Bank Irish Leagues
Fri. 5th to	
Sun. 7th	Guinness PRO14 (13)
	Aviva English Premiership (13)
Sat. 6th	English National Leagues
	BT Scottish National Leagues
	Welsh National Cup (1)
Thu. 11th to	
Sun. 14th	European Champions Cup (5)
	European Challenge Cup (5)
Fri. 12th to	
Sun. 14th	British & Irish Cup (5)
Sat. 13th	Guinness PRO14 (11*)
	English National Leagues
	BT Scottish Premiership (14)
	BT Scottish National Leagues
	Welsh National Championship
	Welsh National Leagues
Thu. 18th to	
Sun. 21st	European Champions Cup (6)
	European Challenge Cup (6)
Sat. 20th	Guinness PRO14 (12*)
	British & Irish Cup (6)
	English National Leagues
	BT Scottish Premiership (15)
	BT Scottish National Leagues
	Welsh National Championship
	Welsh National Leagues
Fri. 26th to	
Sun. 28th	HSBC 7s World Series (Sydney)
	Anglo-Welsh Cup (3)
Sat. 27th	English National Leagues
	BT Scottish Premiership (16)
	BT Scottish National Leagues
	Ulster Bank Irish Leagues
Sat. 27th and	
Sun. 28th	GK IPA Championship (14)

FEBRUARY 2018

Fri. 2nd to	
Sun. 4th	Anglo-Welsh Cup (4)
Sat. 3rd	WALES v SCOTLAND (14:15)
	FRANCE v IRELAND (16:45)
	English National Leagues
	Welsh Principality Premiership (16)
	Ulster Bank Irish Leagues
Sat. 3rd and	
Sun. 4th	HSBC 7s World Series (Hamilton)
Sun. 4th	ITALY v ENGLAND (15:00)
Fri. 9th to	
Sun. 11th	Guinness PRO14 (14)

	Aviva English Premiership (14)
	GK IPA Championship (15)
Sat. 10th	IRELAND v ITALY (14:15)
	ENGLAND v WALES (16:45)
	English National Leagues
	Welsh Principality Premiership (17)
Sun. 11th	SCOTLAND v FRANCE (15:00)
	U20 County Championship (1)
Fri. 16th	Guinness PRO14 (15)
Fri. 16th and	
Sat. 17th	Ulster Bank Irish Leagues
Fri. 16th to	
Sun. 18th	Aviva English Premiership (15)
	GK IPA Championship (16)
Sat.17th	English National Leagues
	BT Scottish Premiership (17)
	BT Scottish National Leagues
	Welsh Principality Premiership (18)
	Welsh National Championship
	Welsh National Leagues
Fri. 23rd	FRANCE v ITALY (20:00)+
Fri. 23rd to	
Sun. 25th	Guinness PRO14 (16)
	Aviva English Premiership (16)
Sat. 24th	IRELAND v WALES (14:15)
	SCOTLAND v ENGLAND (16:45)
	Welsh Principality Premiership (19)
Sun. 25th	U20 County Championship (2)

MARCH 2018

Fri. 2nd and	
Sat. 3rd	Ulster Bank Irish Leagues
Fri. 2nd to	
Sun. 4th	HSBC 7s World Series (L. Vegas)
	Guinness PRO14 (17)
	Aviva English Premiership (17)
Sat. 3rd	English National Leagues
	BT Scottish Premiership (18)
	BT Scottish National Leagues
	Welsh National Championship
	Welsh National Leagues
Sat. 3rd and	
Sun. 4th	GK IPA Championship (17)
Sat. 10th	IRELAND v SCOTLAND (14:15)
	FRANCE v ENGLAND (16:45)
	English National Leagues
	Welsh Principality Premiership (20)
	Welsh National Championship
	Welsh National Leagues
Sat. 10th and	
Sun. 11th	HSBC 7s World Series (V'couver)
Sat. 10th to	
Mon. 12th	Anglo-Welsh Cup SF
Sun. 11th	WALES v ITALY (15:00)
Fri. 16th to	
Sun. 18th	GK IPA Championship (18)
Sat. 17th	ITALY v SCOTLAND (12:30)
	ENGLAND v IRELAND (14:45)
	WALES v FRANCE (17:00)
	Welsh Principality Premiership (21)
Sat. 17th to	
Mon. 19th	Anglo-Welsh Cup Final
Sun. 18th	U20 County Championship (3)

Fri. 23rd to	
Sun. 25th	Guinness PRO14 (18)
	Aviva English Premiership (18)
Sat. 24th	English National Leagues
	BT Scottish National Leagues
	Welsh Principality Premiership (22)
	Welsh National Championship
	Welsh National Leagues
	Ulster Bank Irish Leagues
Sat. 24th and	
Sun. 25th	GK IPA Championship (19)
Mon. 26th	Aviva 'A' League
Thu. 29th to	
Sat. 31st	European Champions Cup QF**
	European Challenge Cup QF**
Fri. 30th	Welsh Principality Premiership (23)
Sat. 31st	BT Scottish National Leagues
	Welsh National Championship
	Welsh National Leagues

APRIL 2018

Sun. 1st	U20 County Championship QF
Mon. 2nd	Aviva 'A' League
	Welsh Principality Premiership (24)
Fri. 6th and	
Sat. 7th	Ulster Bank Irish Leagues
Fri. 6th to	
Sun. 8th	HSBC 7s World Series (H. Kong)
	Guinness PRO14 (19)
	Aviva English Premiership (19)
	GK IPA Championship (20)
Sat. 7th	English National Leagues
	BT Scottish National Leagues
	Welsh Principality Premiership (25)
	Welsh National Leagues
Mon. 9th	Aviva 'A' League
Wed. 11th	BUCS Finals (Twickenham)**
Fri. 13th and	
Sat. 14th	GK IPA Championship (21)
Fri. 13th to	
Sun. 15th	Guinness PRO14 (20)
	Aviva English Premiership (20)
Sat. 14th	English National Leagues
	Welsh Principality Premiership (26)
	Ulster Bank Irish Leagues
Sun. 15th	U20 County Championship SF
Mon. 16th	Aviva 'A' League
Fri. 20th to	
Sun. 22nd	European Champions Cup SF**
	European Challenge Cup SF**
Sat. 21st	English National Leagues
	Welsh Principality Premiership (27)
Mon. 23rd	Aviva 'A' League SF
Fri. 27th and	
Sat. 28th	GK IPA Championship (22)
Fri. 27th to	
Sun. 29th	Guinness PRO14 (21)
	Aviva English Premiership (21)
Sat. 28th	English National Leagues
Sat. 28th and	
Sun. 29th	HSBC 7s World Series (S'pore)
	Women's County Ch'ship (1)
Mon. 30th	Aviva 'A' League Final

MAY 2018

Fri. 4th to	
Sun. 6th	Guinness PRO14 QF**
Sat. 5th	Aviva English Premiership (22)
	Welsh Principality Premiership (28)
	County Championship (1)
	Army v Royal Navy
	(Babcock Trophy – Twickenham)
Sun. 6th	RFU Junior Vase Final
	RFU Senior Vase Final
	RFU Intermediate Cup Final
	Women's County Ch'ship (2)
Fri. 11th	European Challenge Cup Final
	(Bilbao)
Sat. 12th	European Champions Cup Final
	(Bilbao)
	County Championship (2)
	Welsh Principality Premiership (29)
Sun. 13th	Women's County Ch'ship (3)
Fri. 18th and	
Sat. 19th	Aviva English Premiership SF**
Fri. 18th to	
Sun. 20th	Guinness PRO14 SF**
Sat. 19th	County Championship (3)
Sun. 20th	Women's County Ch'ship SF
Sat. 26th	Guinness PRO14 Final
	Aviva English Premiership Final
Sat. 26th and	
Sun. 27th	HSBC 7s World Series (Paris)
Sun. 27th	ENGLAND v Barbarians
	County Championship Finals
	Women's County Ch'ship Finals
	U20 County Championship Finals

JUNE 2018

Sat. 2nd and	
Sun. 3rd	HSBC 7s World Series (London)

Note
At the time of going to press, fixture dates for some cup competitions were unavailable beyond the early rounds or group/pool stages.

Key
TRC = The Rugby Championship
BC = Bledisloe Cup
FC = Freedom Cup
MCP = Mandela Challenge Plate
tbc = to be confirmed
* fixtures outstanding from earlier rounds
** dates and times to be confirmed
+ venue to be announced